ED EMBERLEY'S B[   ]BOOK

LITTLE, BROWN AND COMPA[   ]TORONTO

IN PRAISE OF PRÁTAÍ (POTATOES)

THIS BOOK IS DEDICATED TO THE PRÁTA (PRAY-TEE).
FOR WITHOUT IT MY IRISH GREAT GRANDFATHER MIGHT NEVER
HAVE SURVIVED THE GREAT FAMINE IN IRELAND (SO THEY
SAY) TO FOUND A FAMILY IN THE NEW WORLD · · ·

NO PRÁTA, NO GREAT GRANDFATHER.
NO GREAT GRANDFATHER, NO FAMILY
NO FAMILY, NO ED EMBERLEY
NO ED EMBERLEY, NO BIG,
GREEN
DRAWING
BOOK!
SO IF YOU LIKE THIS BOOK I HOPE YOU WILL RESERVE
SOME OF YOUR KIND THOUGHTS FOR THE HUMBLE
TUBER WITHOUT WHOSE HELP THIS BOOK MIGHT
NEVER HAVE BEEN.

Ed Emberley

LIBRARY of CONGRESS CATALOGING in PUBLICATION DATA

EMBERLEY, ED.
    ED EMBERLEY'S BIG GREEN DRAWING BOOK.

    SUMMARY: STEP-BY-STEP INSTRUCTIONS FOR DRAWING
PEOPLE AND ANIMALS USING A MINIMUM OF LINE AND
CIRCLE COMBINATIONS.

    1. DRAWING -- TECHNIQUE -- JUVENILE LITERATURE.
[1. DRAWING -- TECHNIQUE] I. TITLE. II. BIG
GREEN DRAWING BOOK.
NC670.E45   741.2'6   79-16247
ISBN 0-316-23595-4
ISBN 0-316-23596-2 PBK.
    HC: 20 19 18 17 16 15 14 13 12 11
    PB: 20 19 18 17 16 15 14 13

PUBLISHED SIMULTANEOUSLY IN CANADA BY LITTLE, BROWN AND COMPANY LIMITED (CANADA)
PRINTED IN THE UNITED STATES OF AMERICA

HOW TO DRAW *PRÁTA PEOPLE

*PRÁTA (PRAY-TEE), AN OLD IRISH NAME
FOR THE POTATO.
TWO CIRCLES PUT TOGETHER
LOOK SOMETHING LIKE A POTATO

1

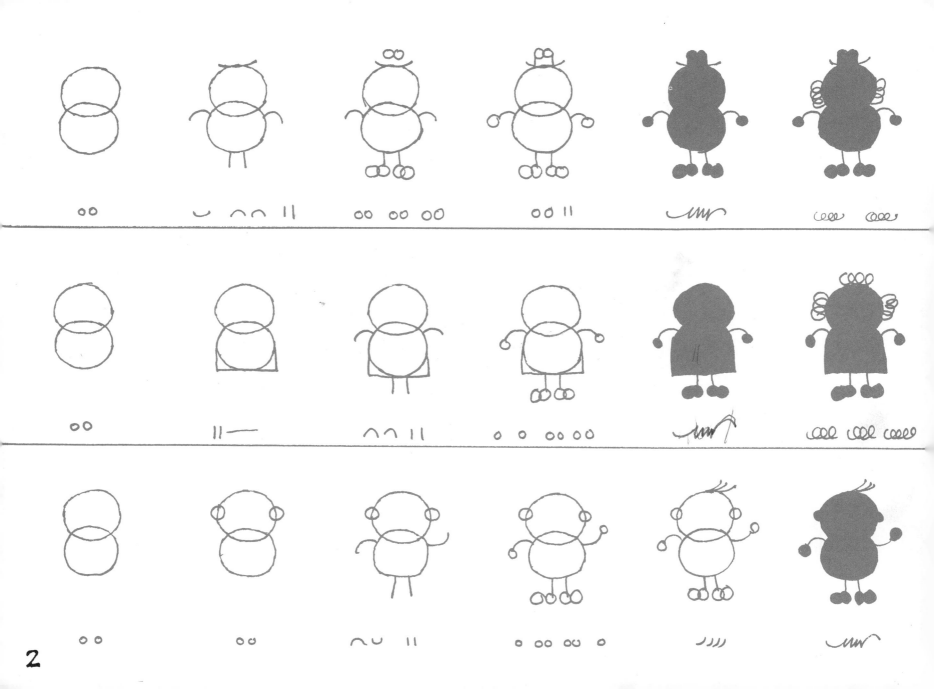

2

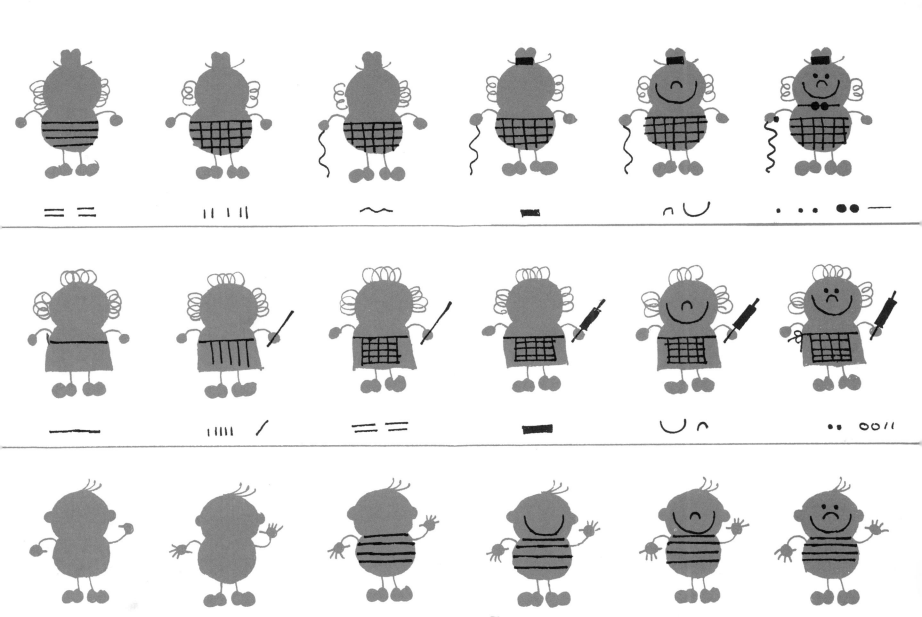

3

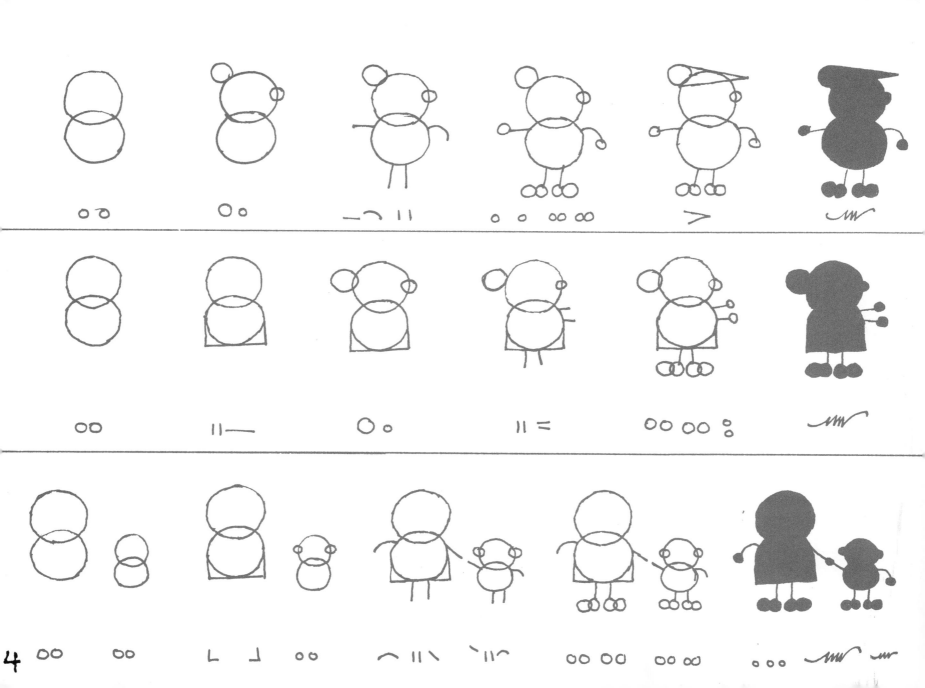

4

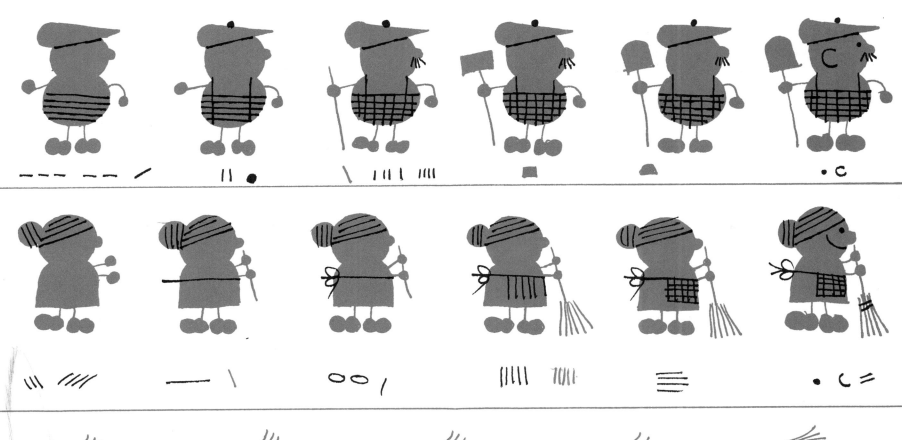

5

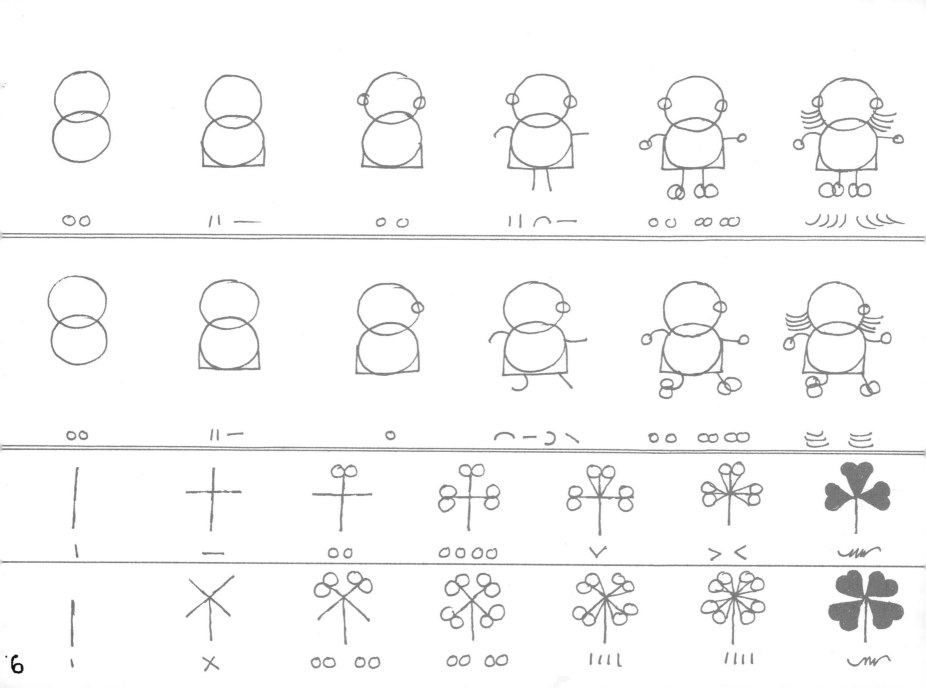

6

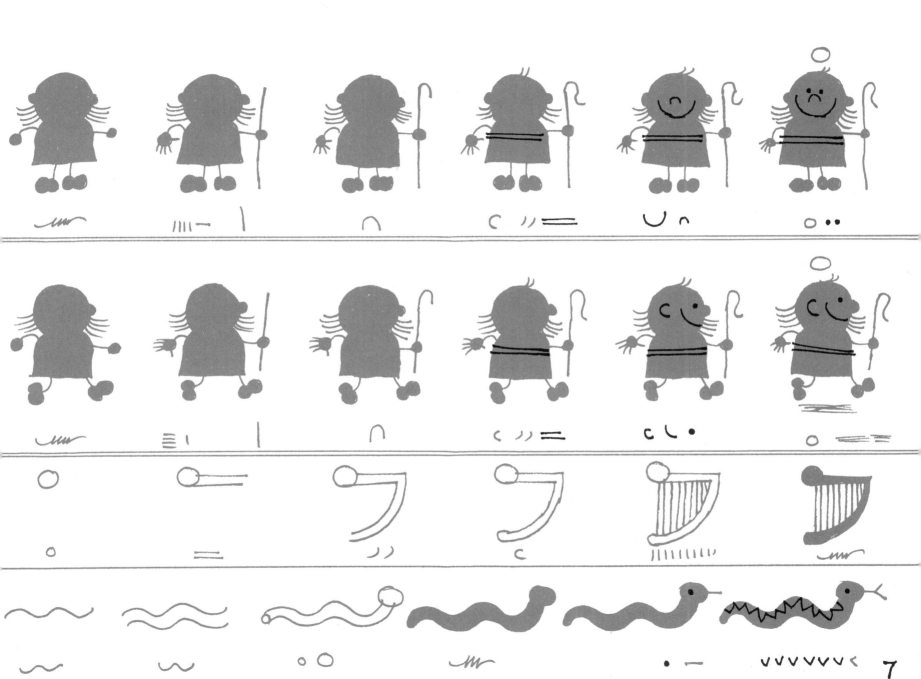

7

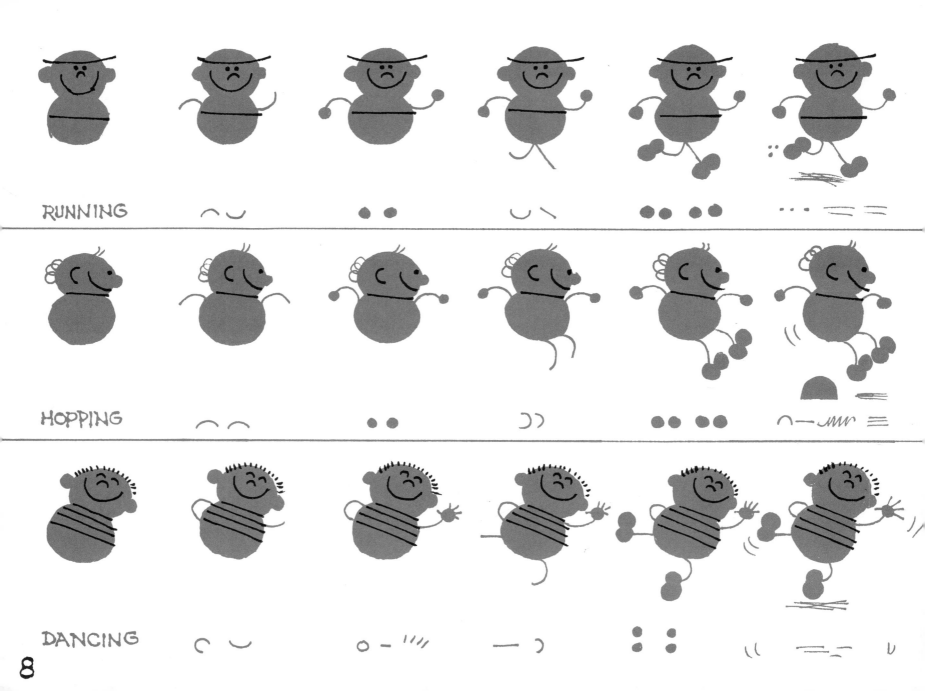

RUNNING

HOPPING

DANCING

8

WALKING

TOOTING   FIDDLER   SWIMMING   SINGING   KICKING   BACK VIEW

LOOKING UP   WORRIED   WINKING   LAUGHING   WEEPING   WHISTLER   GRUMPY

MMM

HUMMING   FRIGHTENED   SLY   SURPRISED   SINGING   BLACK EYE   GLASSES

9

PRATA PONIES

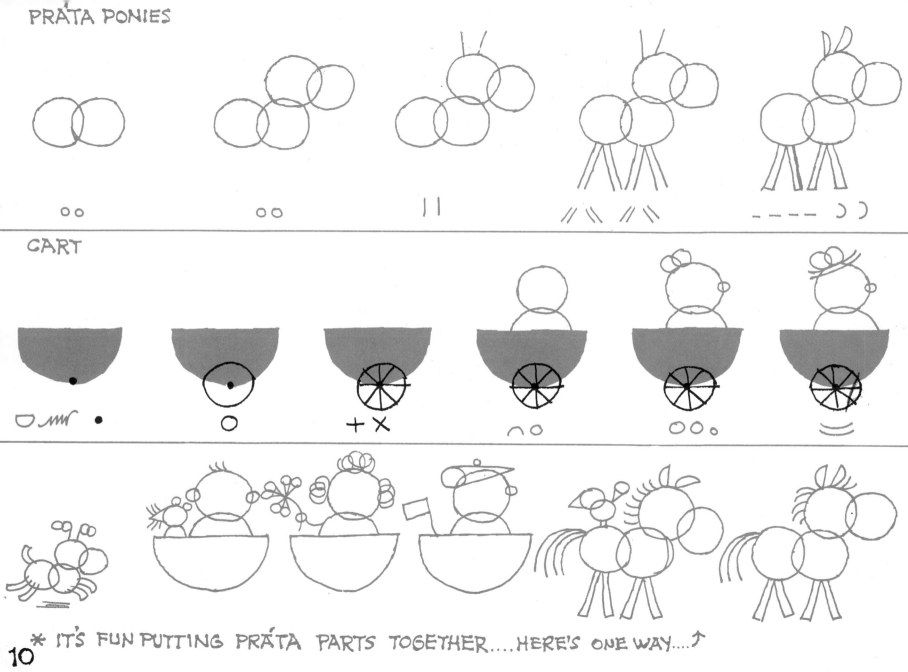

CART

10* IT'S FUN PUTTING PRÁTA PARTS TOGETHER....HERE'S ONE WAY....↑

PRÁTA PONIES DON'T NEED REINS... YOU JUST HAVE TO SAY PLEASE.

17

MORE PRÁTA PONIES

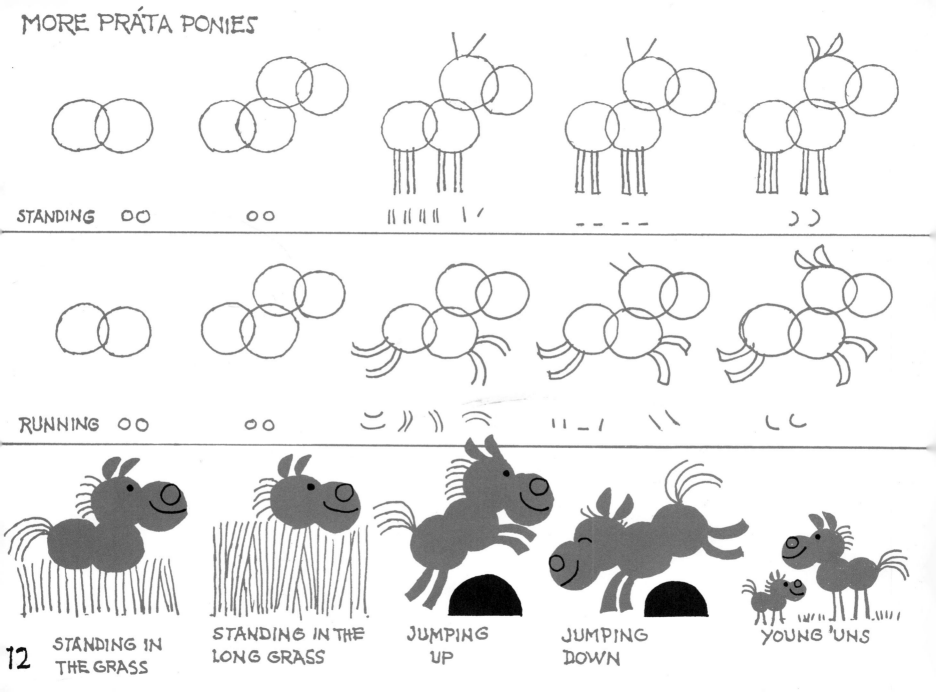

STANDING OO   OO |||||| |/   — — — —   ))

RUNNING OO   OO   ⌐)))) ≈ || —/   \\   L L

STANDING IN THE GRASS

STANDING IN THE LONG GRASS

JUMPING UP

JUMPING DOWN

YOUNG 'UNS

12

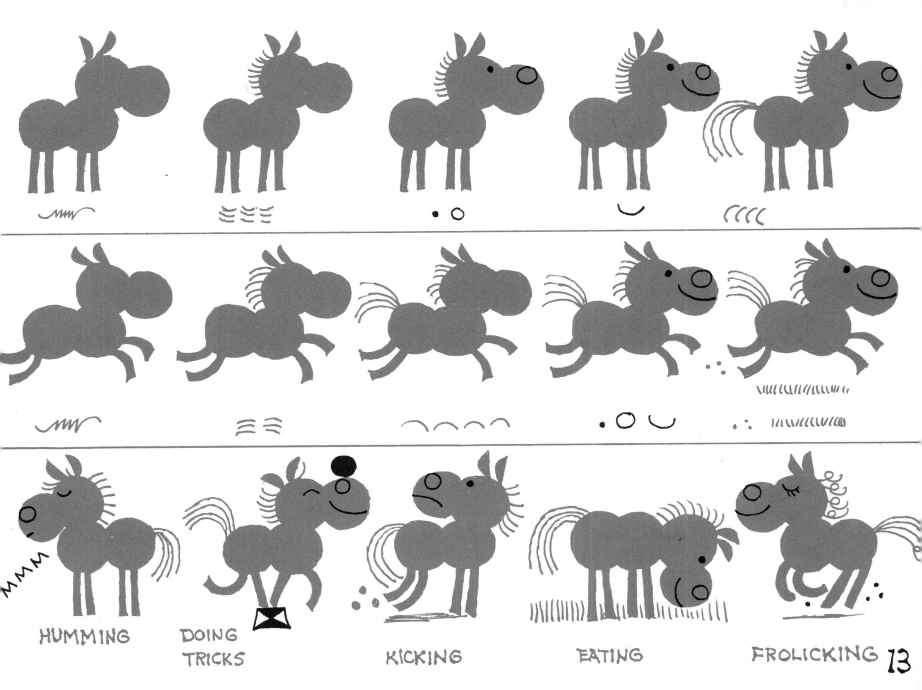

HUMMING

DOING TRICKS

KICKING

EATING

FROLICKING 13

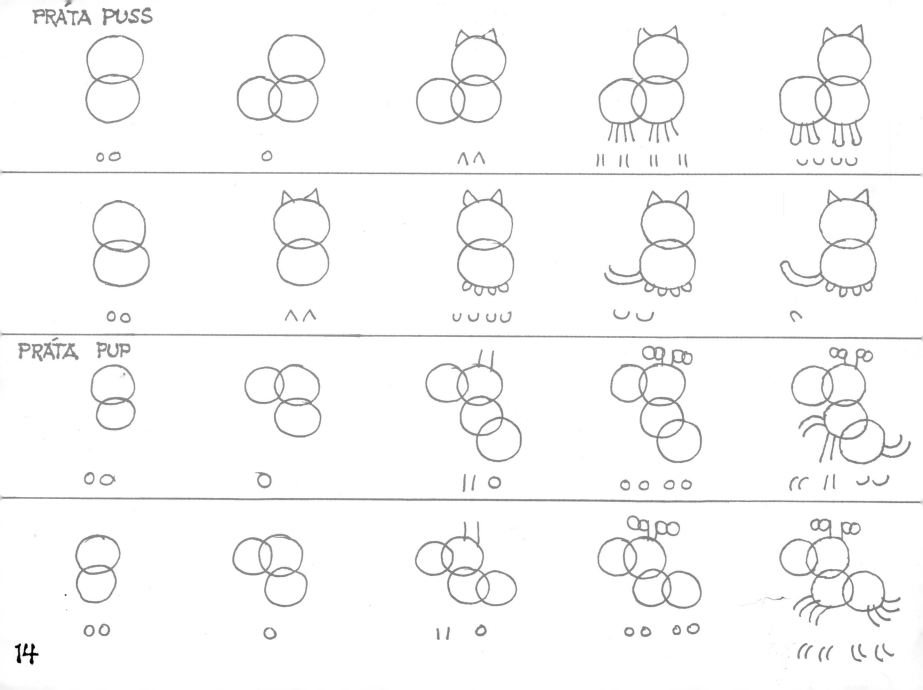

PRÁTA PUSS

PRÁTA PUP

14

WINKING

* IF YOU LOOK AT THE HORSE PAGES YOU WILL SEE SOME OTHER ANIMAL ACTION HINTS.

WEE CRITTERS

PRÁTA PEACOCK

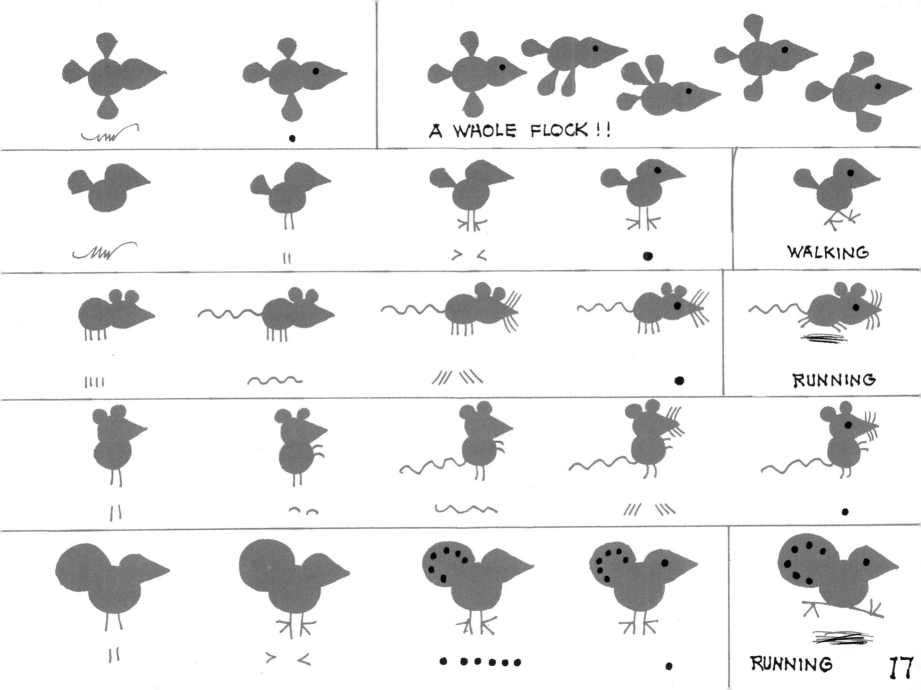

A WHOLE FLOCK !!

WALKING

RUNNING

RUNNING   17

3 WILD'UNS

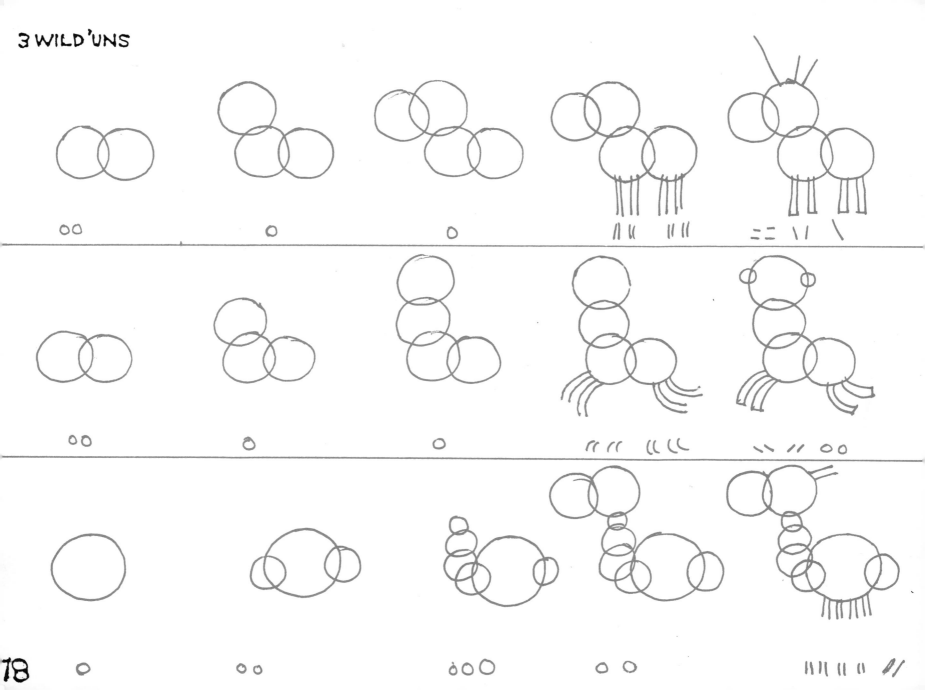

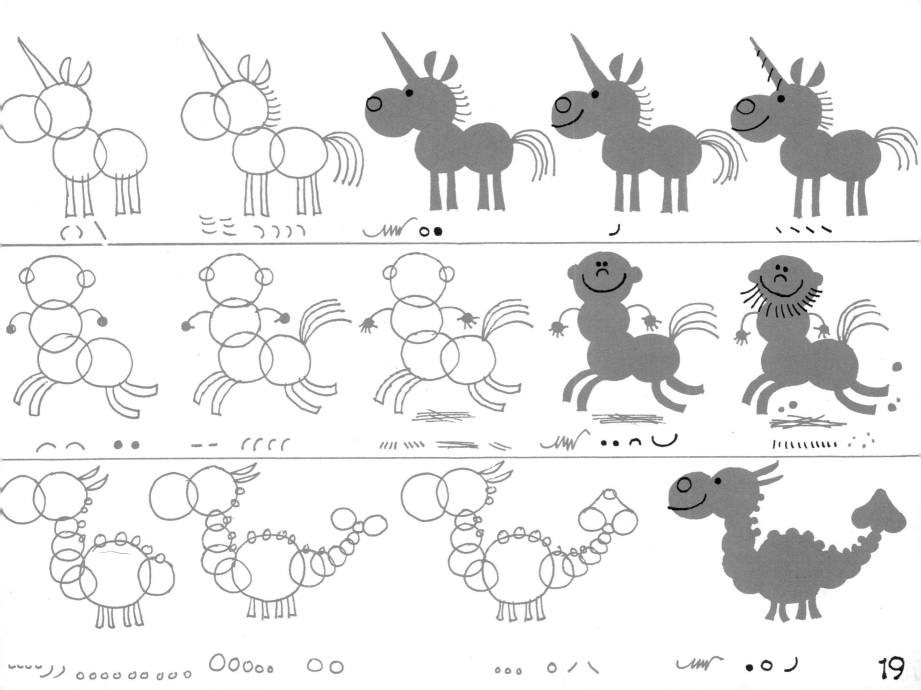

19

PRÁTA PIG

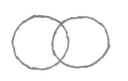 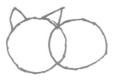 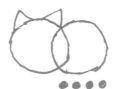    

BUTTERFLY

PRÁTA PEDE

LOTS OF OTHER THINGS CAN BE USED TO MAKE YOUR OWN ANIMATED VEGETATION... SUCH AS:

STRING BEAN FRONT VIEW

SIDE VIEW →

(BANANAS?)

PEAS CORPS { OR GRAPES, OR ORANGES ? }

PEAR E. MASON { APPLES? PICKLES? PEANUTS?? }

20

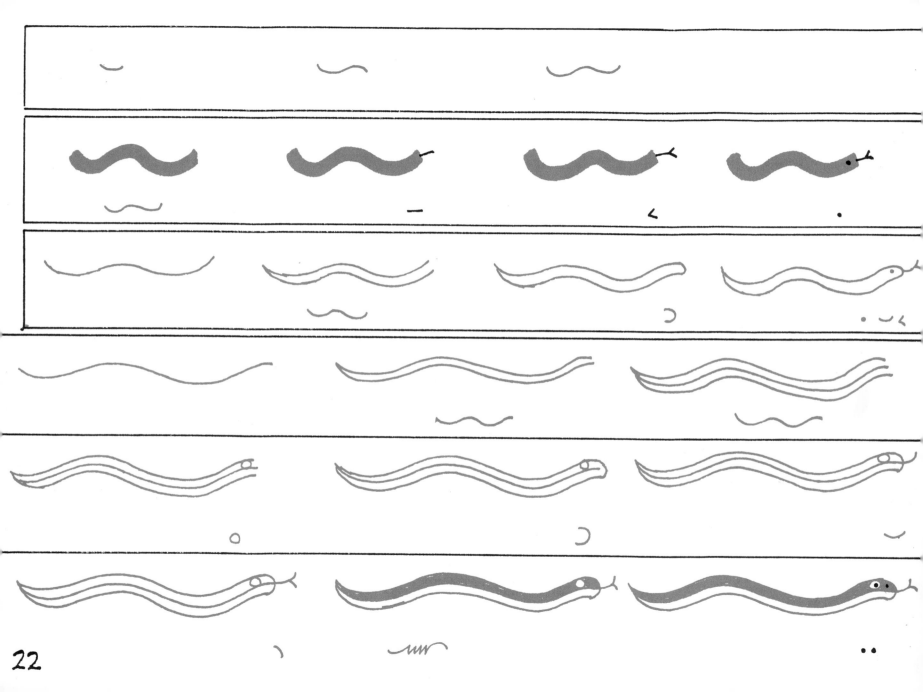

22

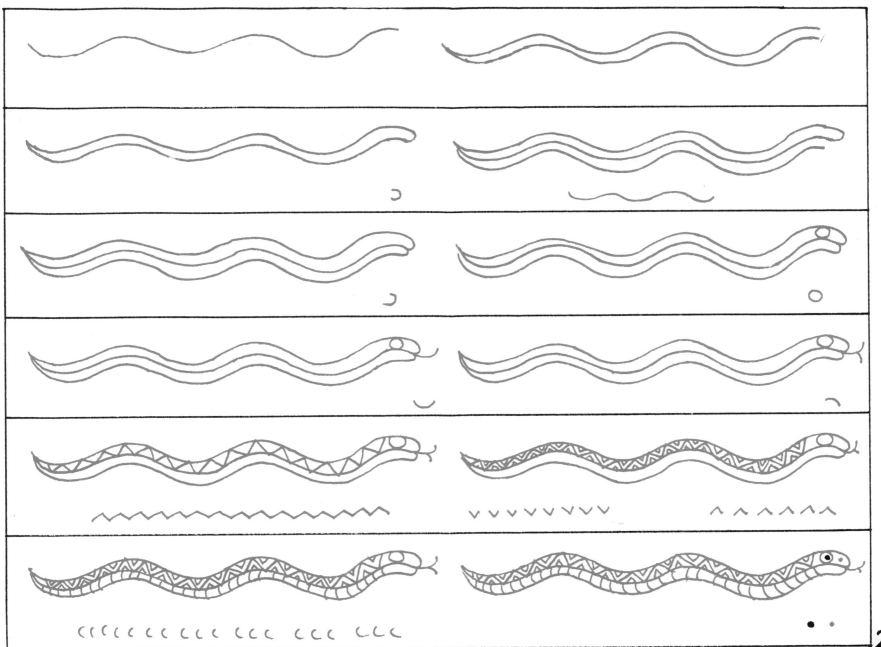

23

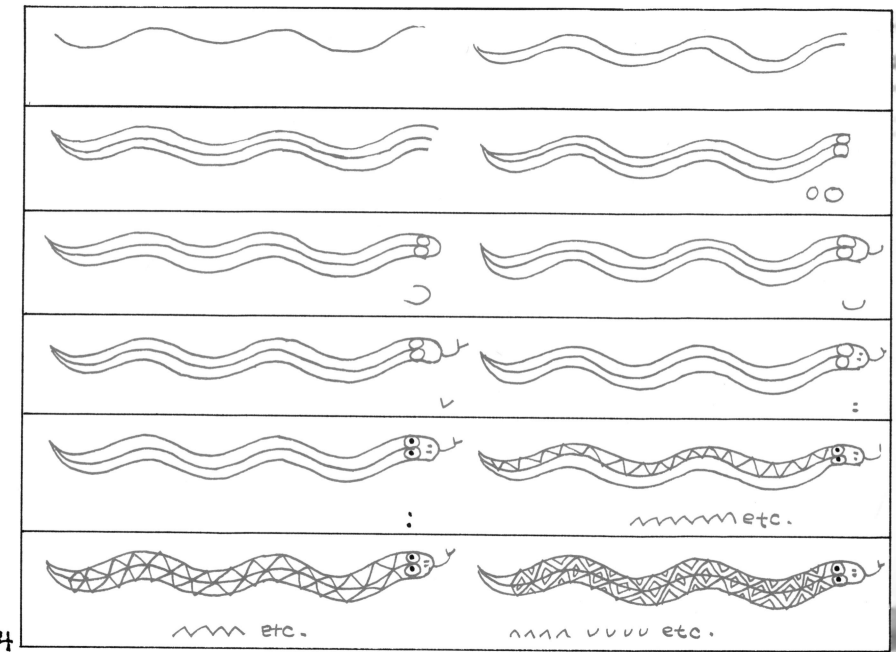

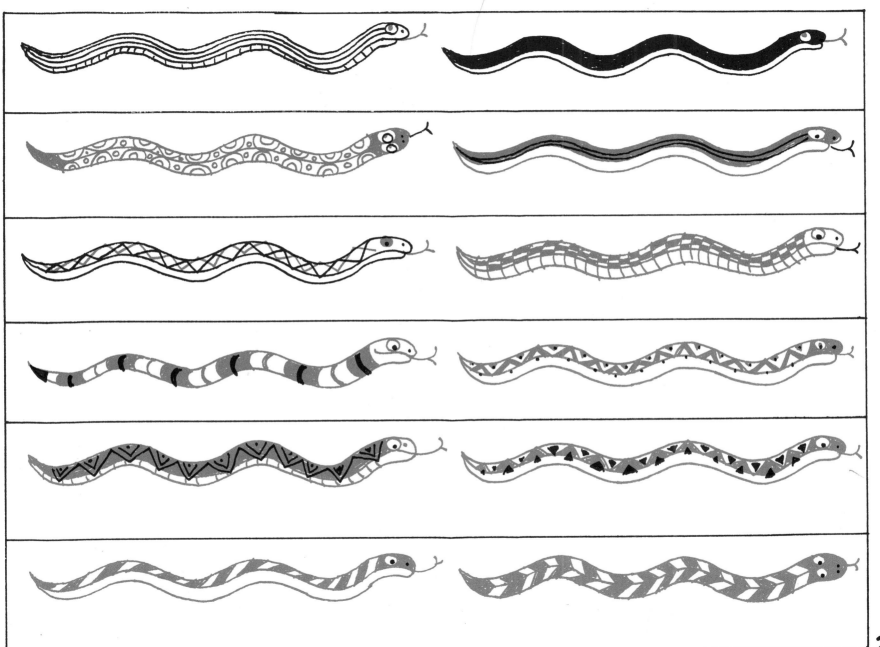

25

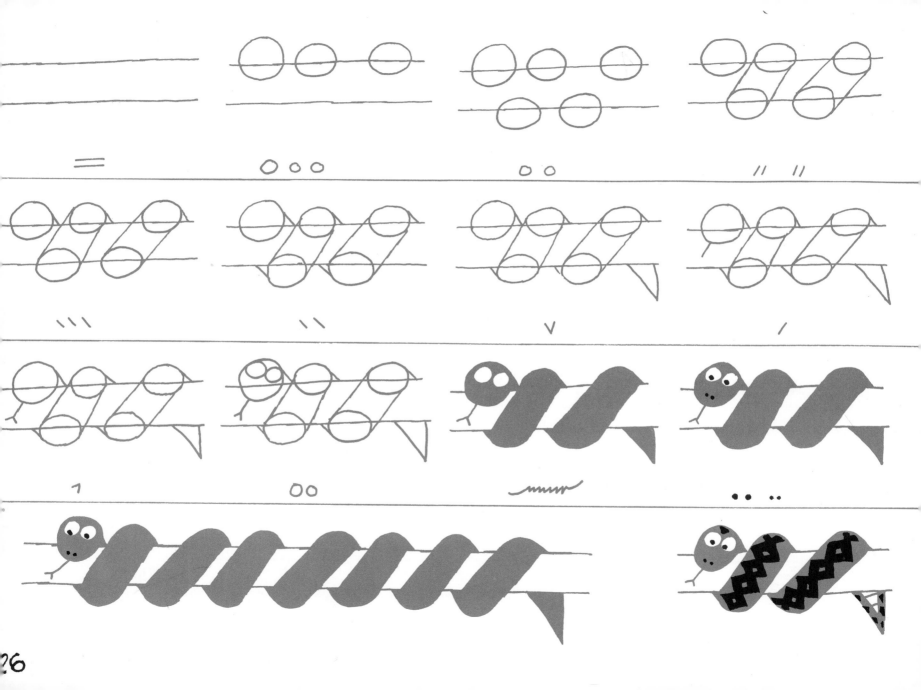

etc.

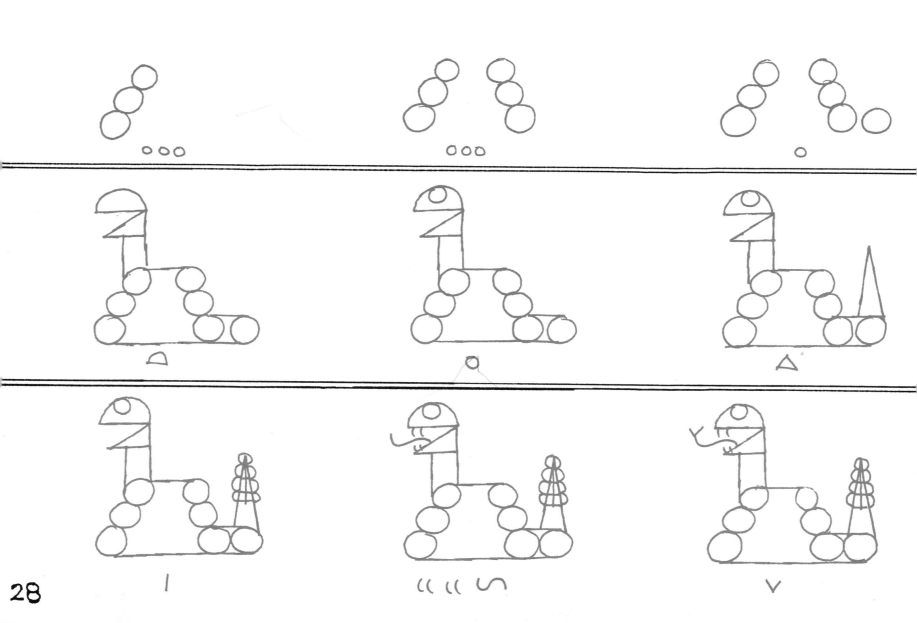

28

29

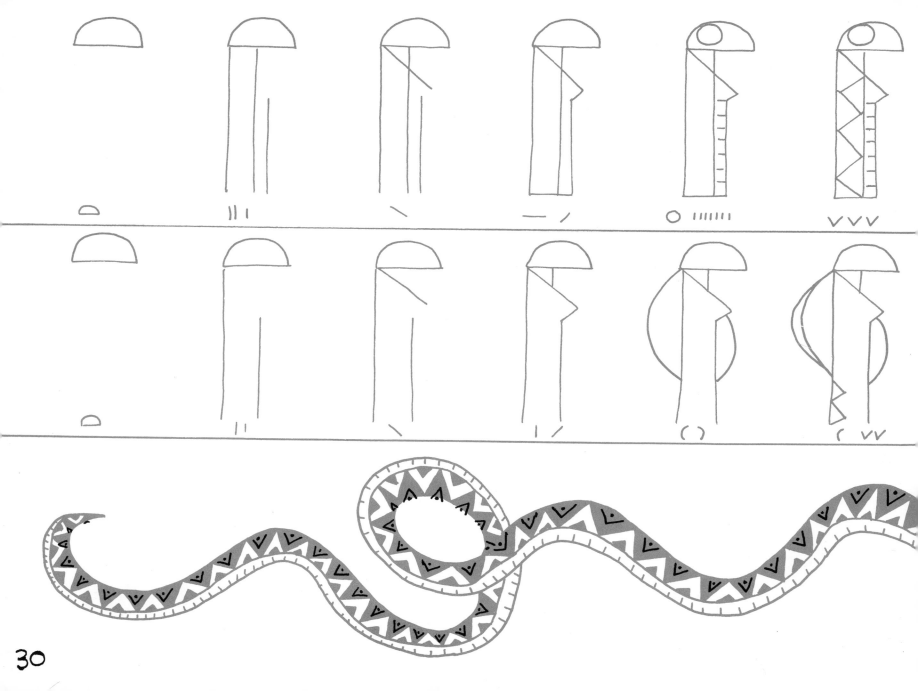

30

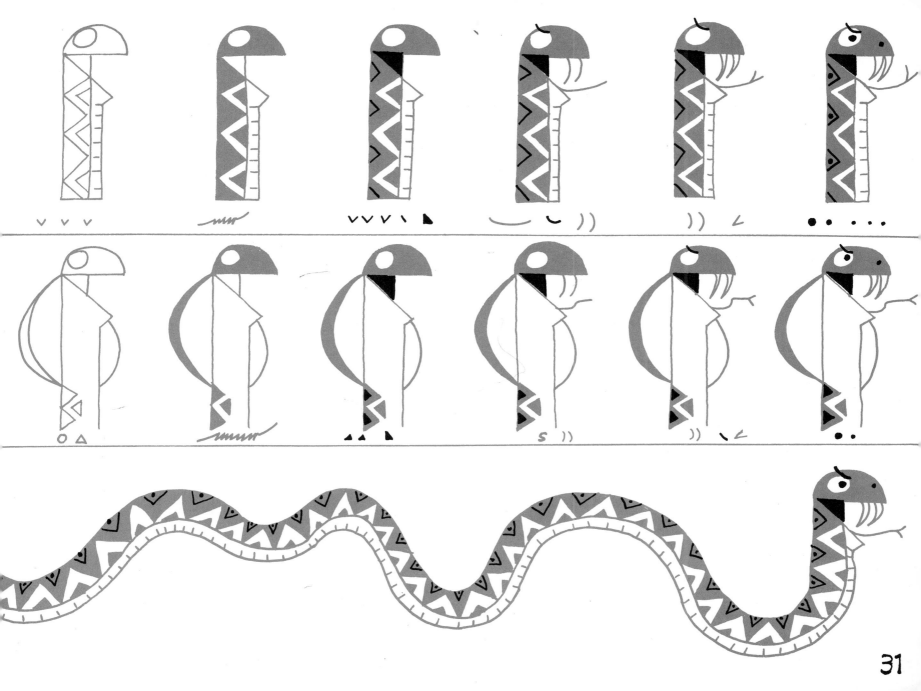

31

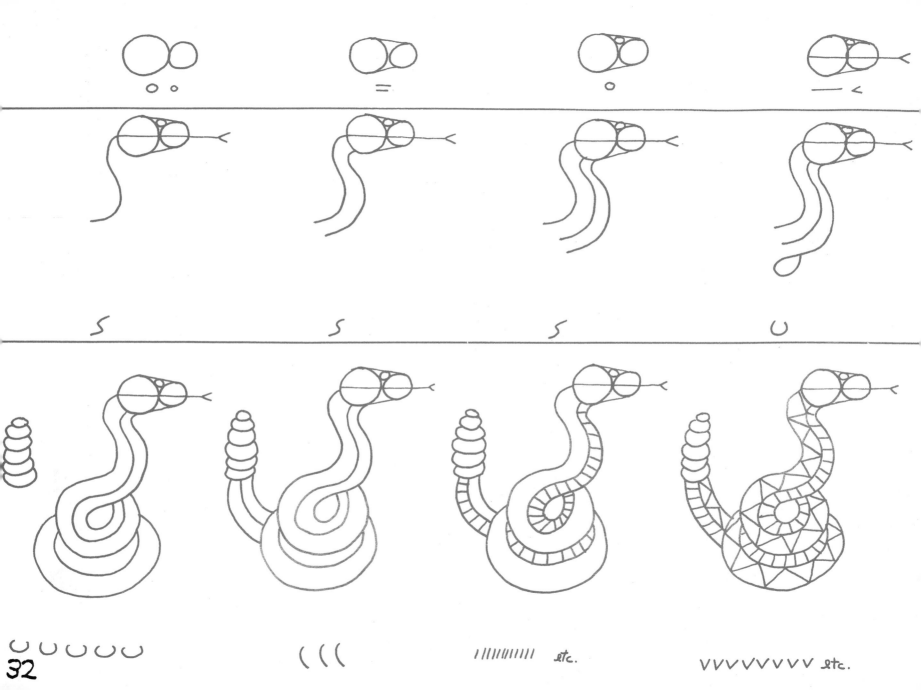

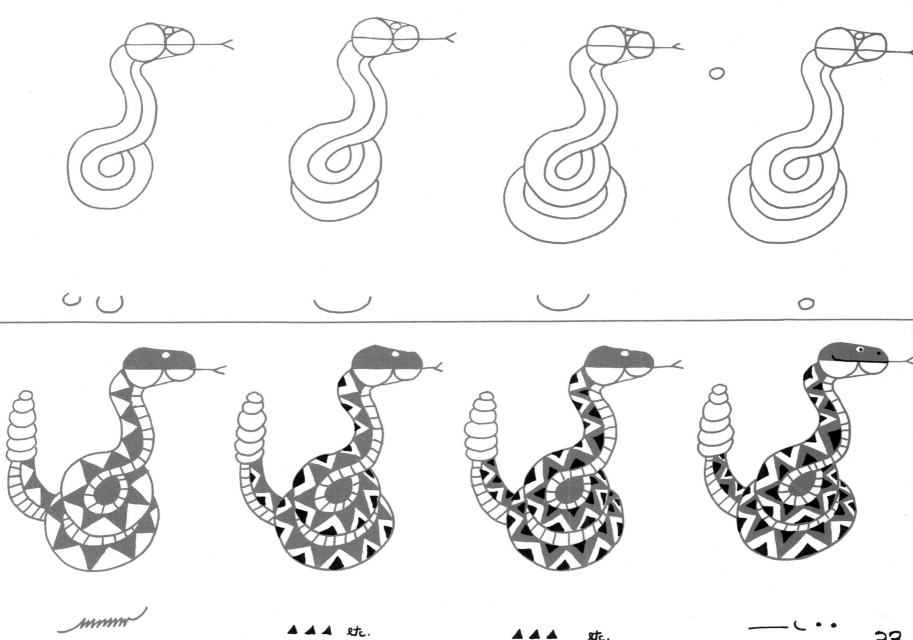

33

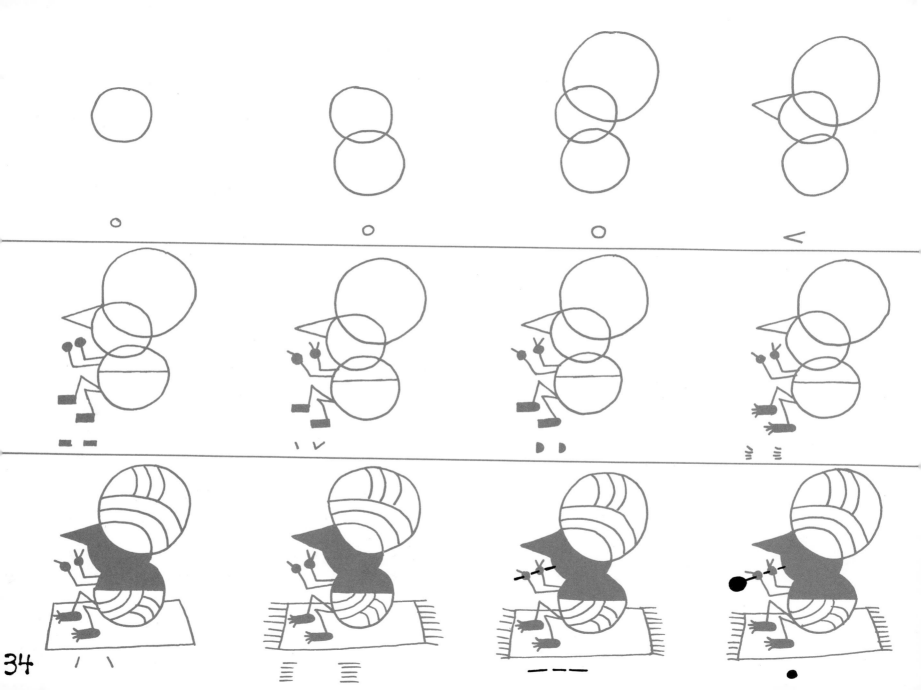

34

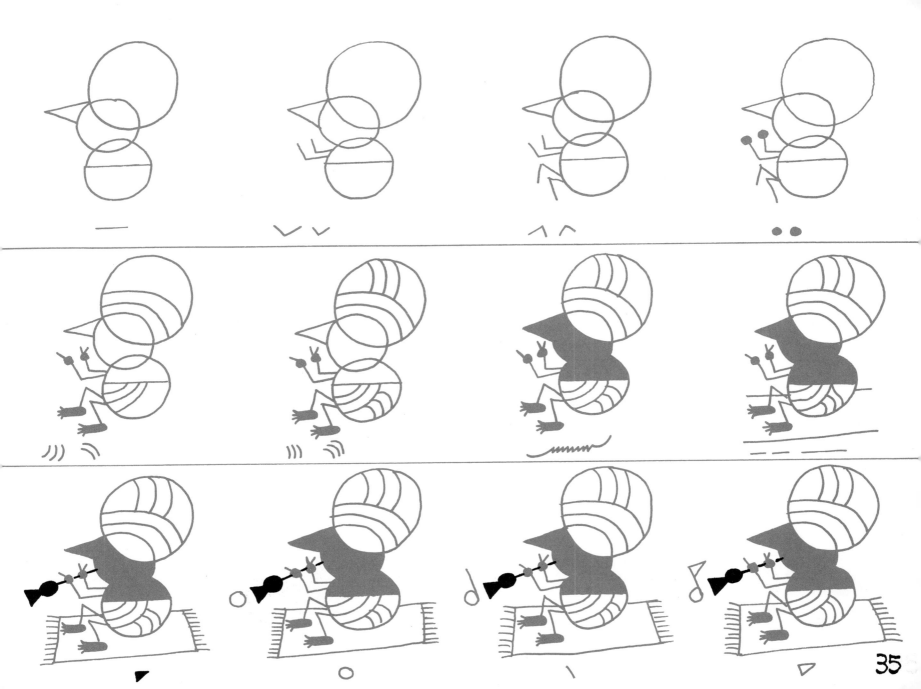

35

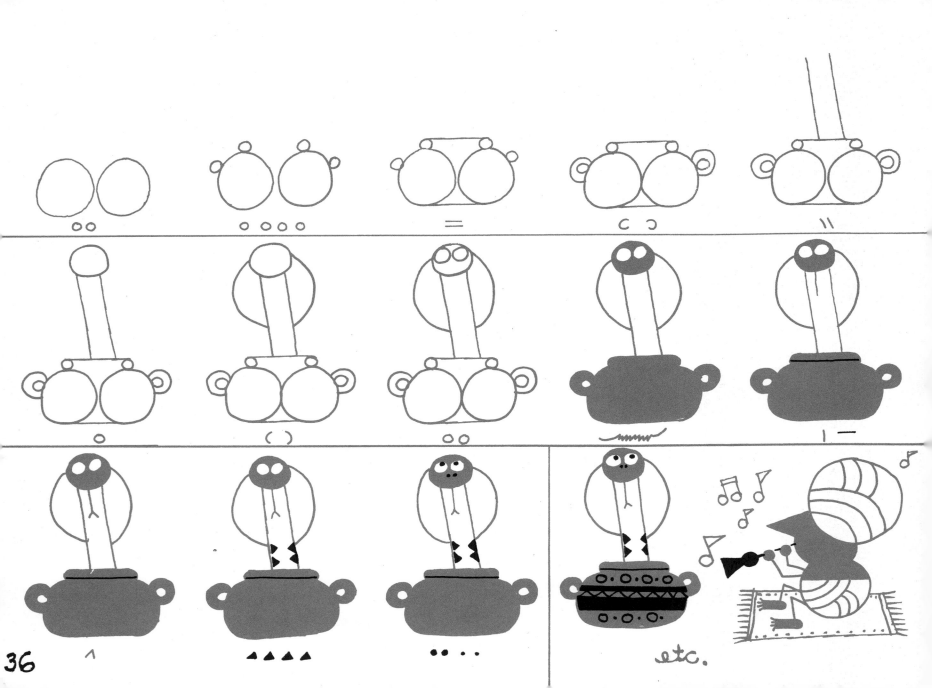

36

etc.

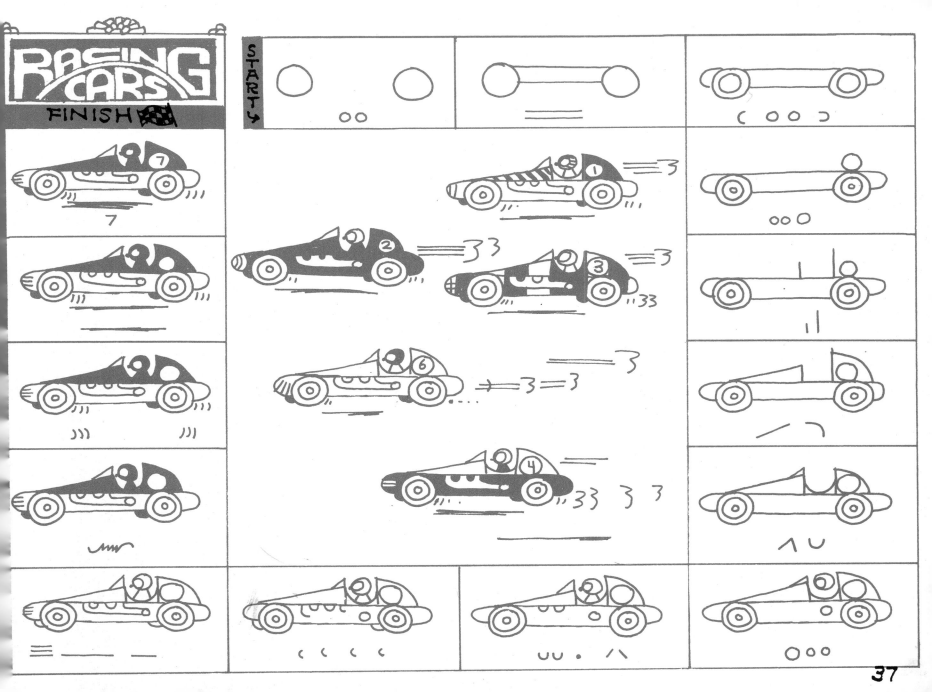

RACING CARS

FINISH

START

37

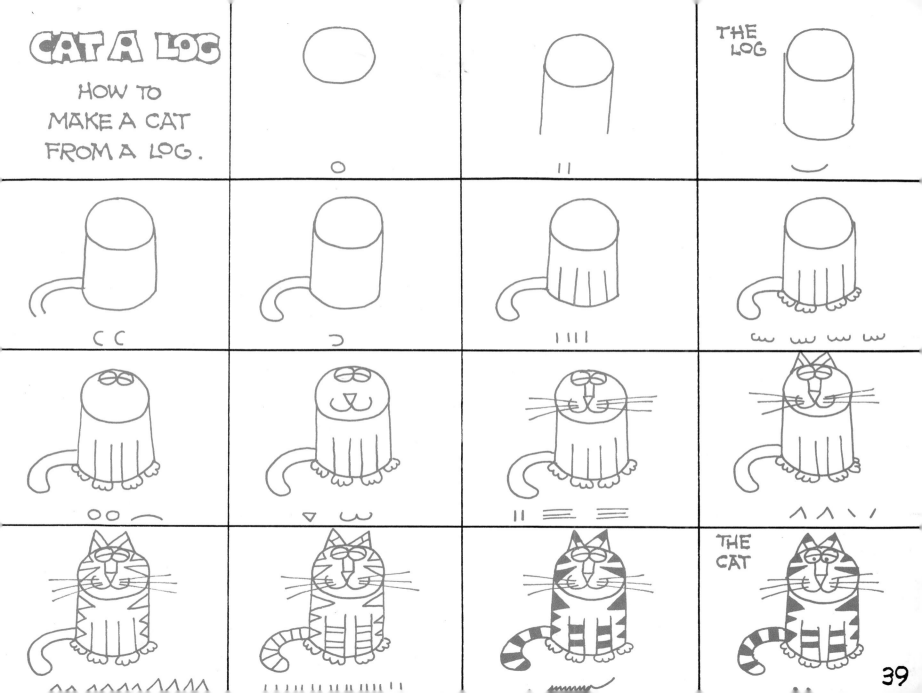

CAT A LOG

HOW TO MAKE A CAT FROM A LOG.

THE LOG

THE CAT

39

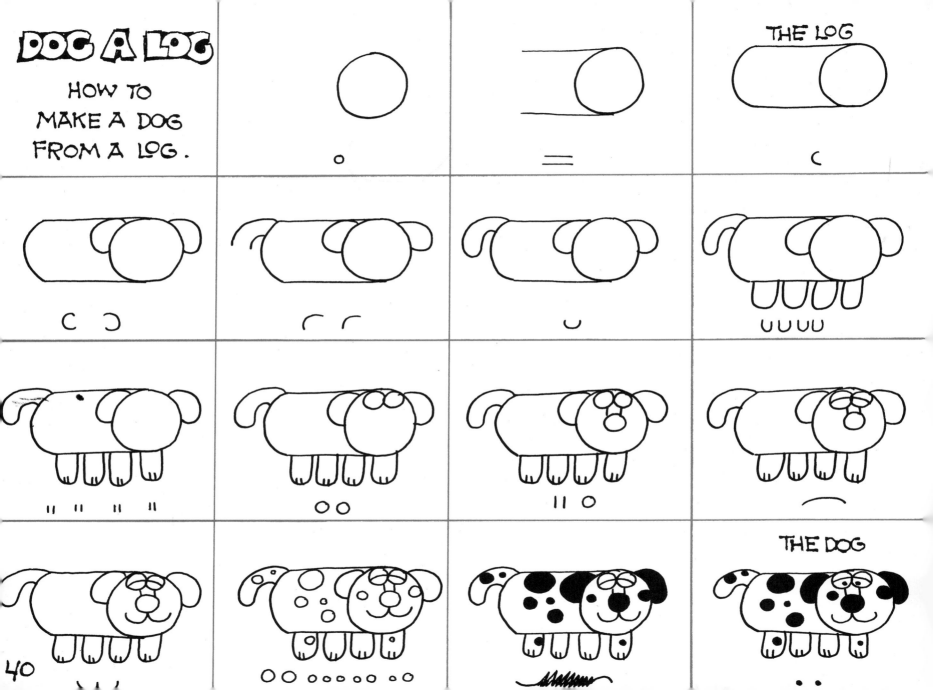

DOG A LOG

HOW TO
MAKE A DOG
FROM A LOG.

THE LOG

THE DOG

40

DOG A LOG

HOW TO MAKE A DOG FROM A LOG.

THE LOG

THE DOG

43

*CROCOLATORS

*GREAT GREEN BEASTS...
HALF ALLIGATOR. HALF CROCODILE!!

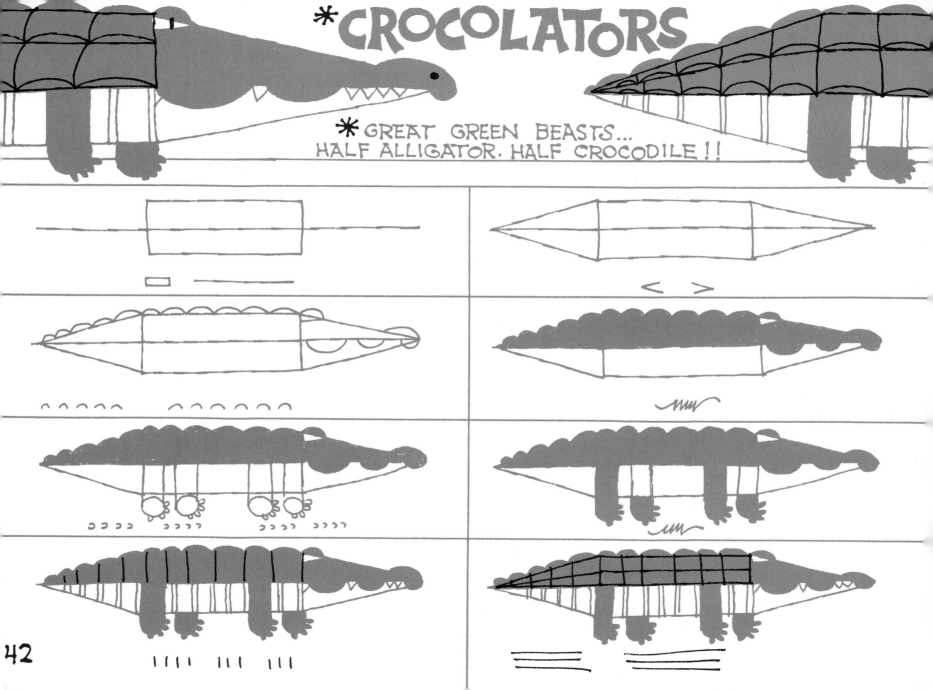

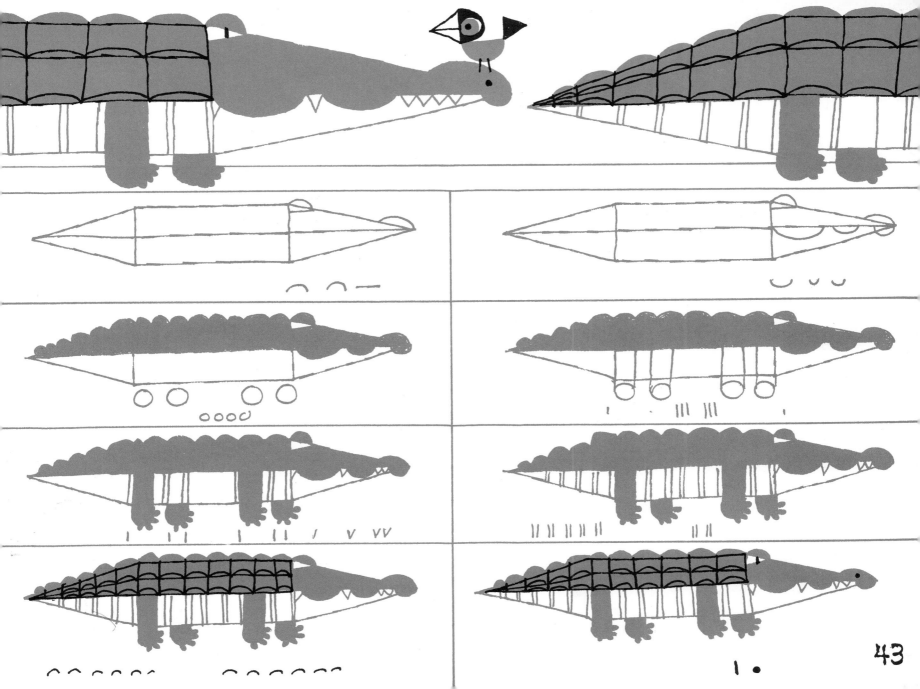

43

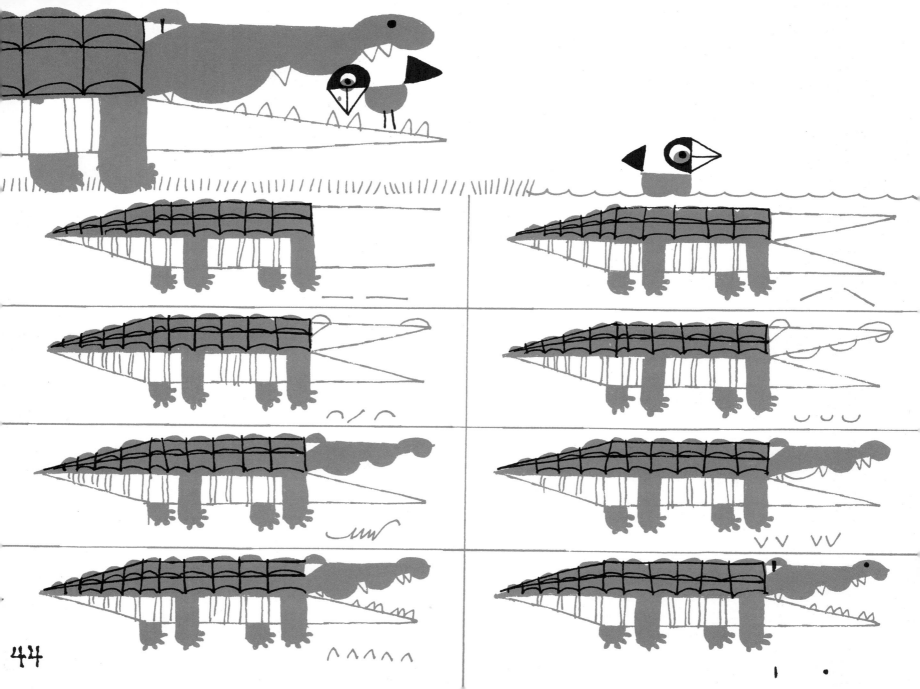

44

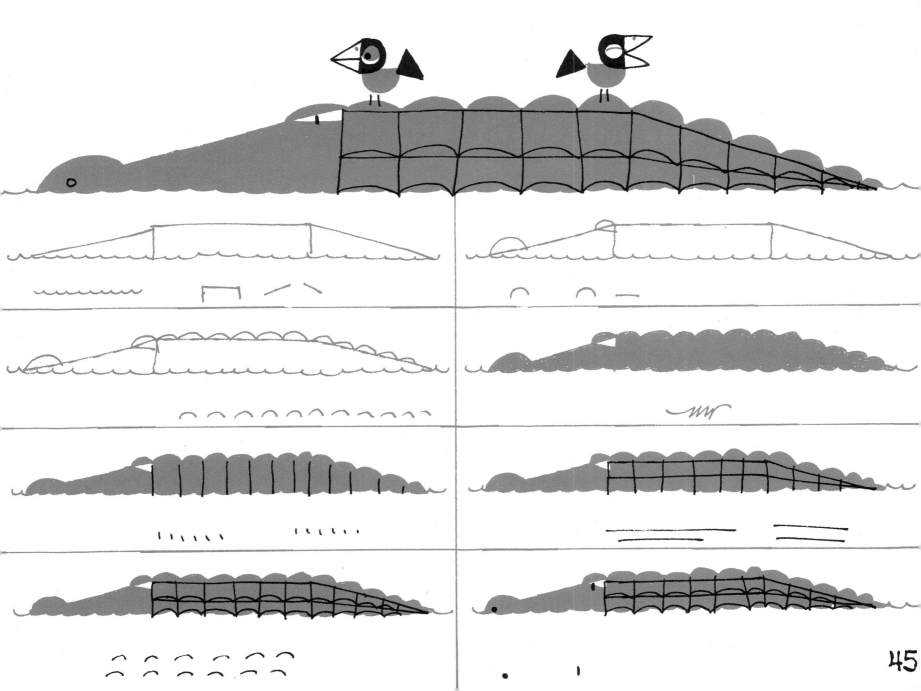

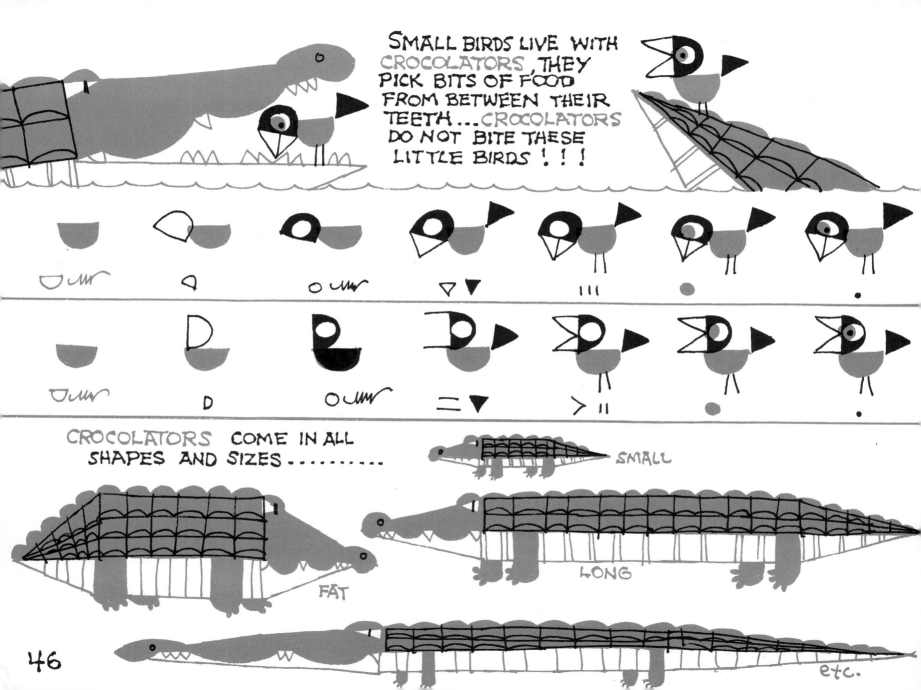

SMALL BIRDS LIVE WITH CROCOLATORS. THEY PICK BITS OF FOOD FROM BETWEEN THEIR TEETH... CROCOLATORS DO NOT BITE THESE LITTLE BIRDS ! ! !

CROCOLATORS COME IN ALL SHAPES AND SIZES..........

SMALL

FAT

LONG

etc.

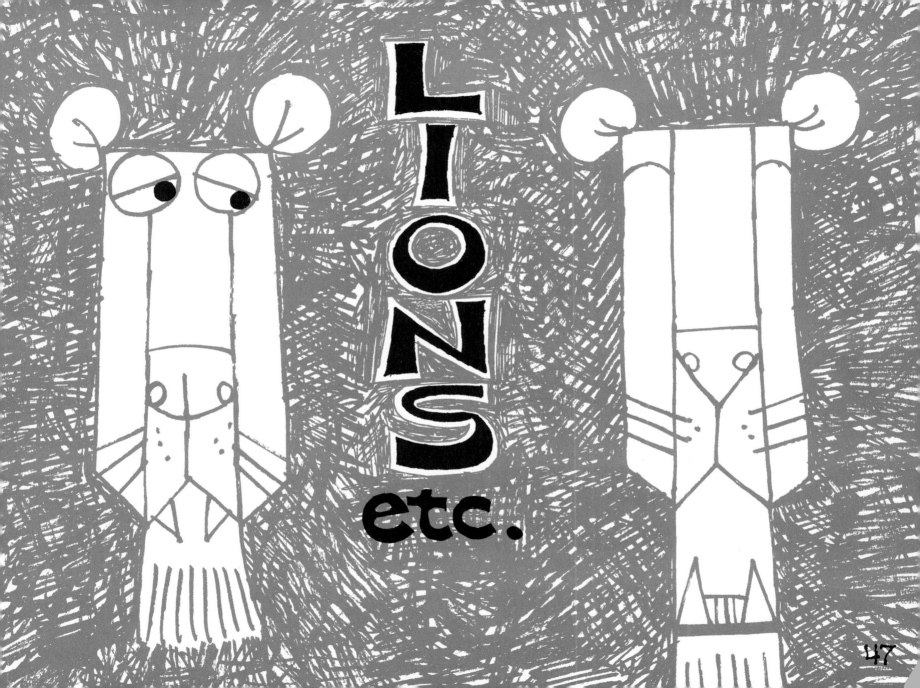

LIONS

etc.

47

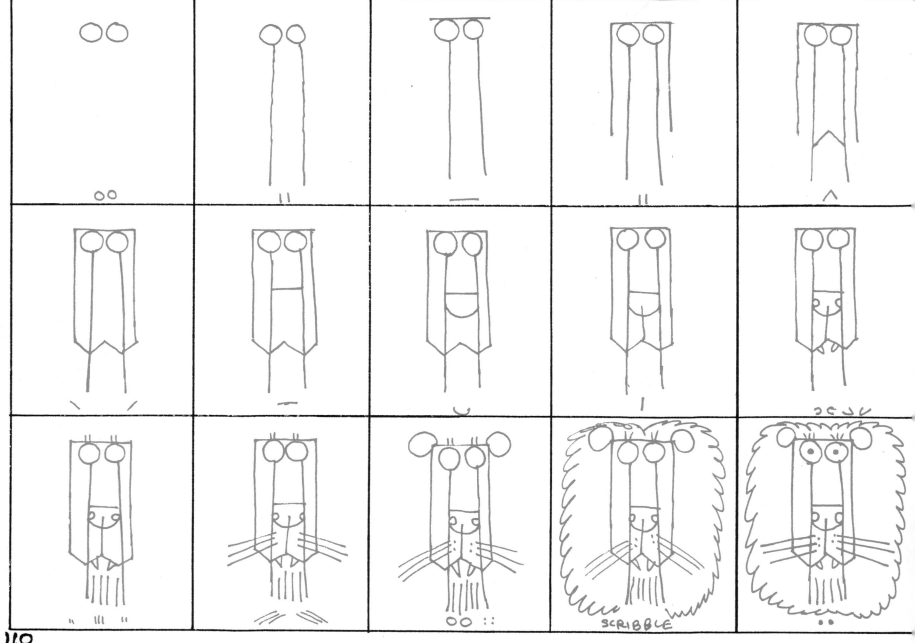

SCRIBBLE

48

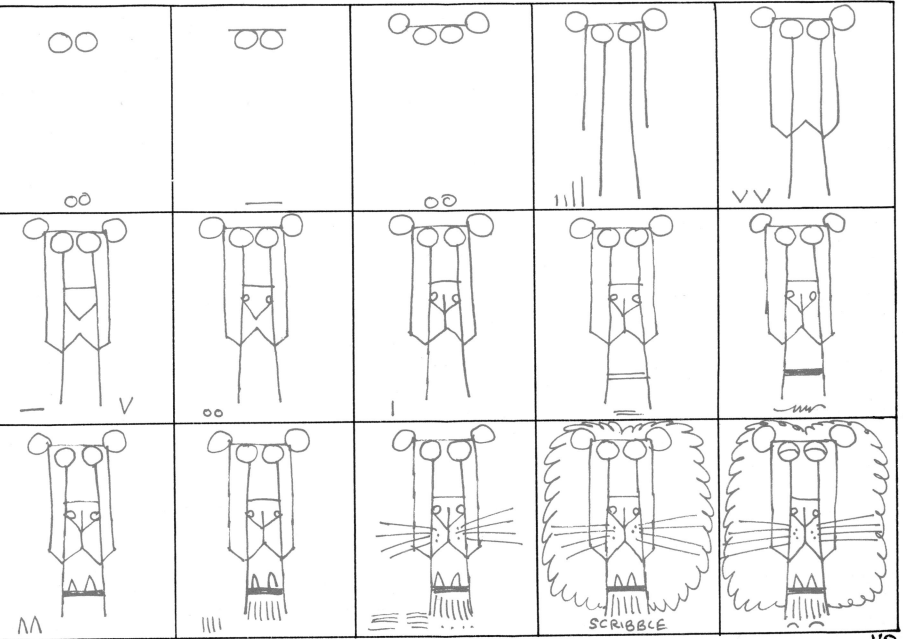

SCRIBBLE

49

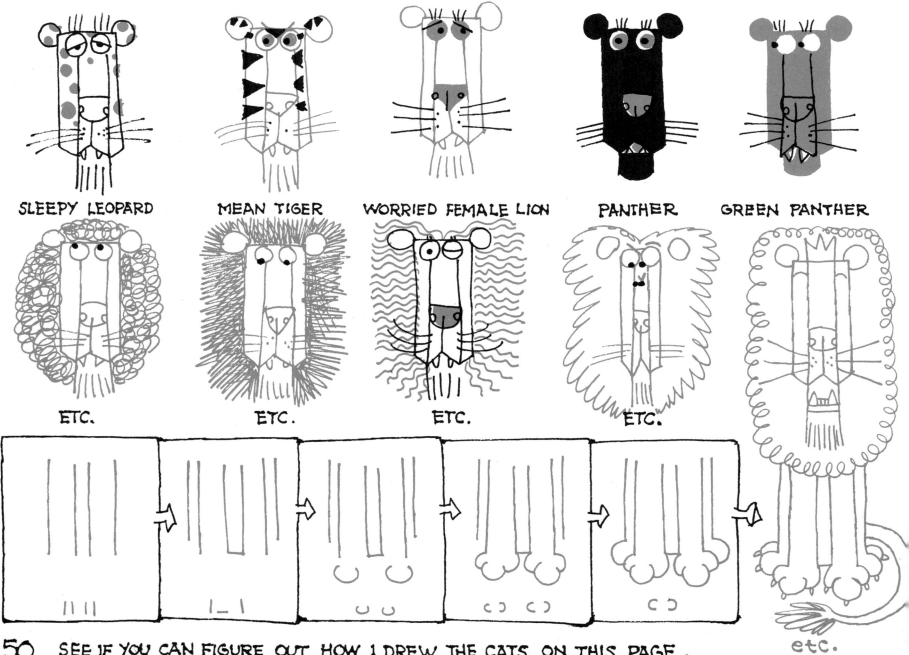

SLEEPY LEOPARD   MEAN TIGER   WORRIED FEMALE LION   PANTHER   GREEN PANTHER

ETC.   ETC.   ETC.   ETC.

etc.

50   SEE IF YOU CAN FIGURE OUT HOW I DREW THE CATS ON THIS PAGE.

TURTLE

I III

II   II

- - - - △○

HAND STUFF

FIRST DRAW A LINE
AROUND YOUR HAND...

52

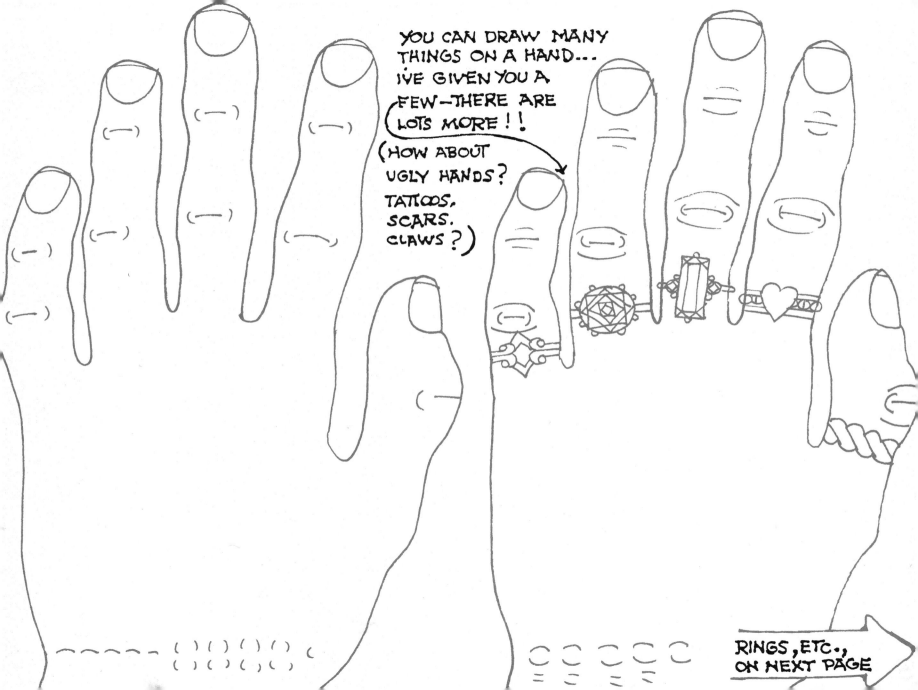

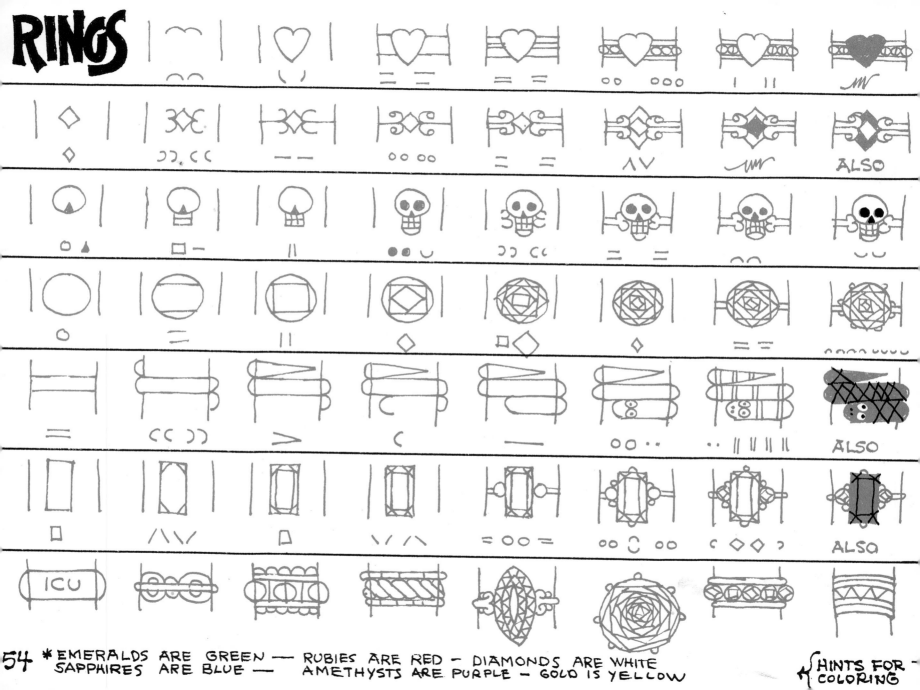

RINGS

54 *EMERALDS ARE GREEN — RUBIES ARE RED — DIAMONDS ARE WHITE
SAPPHIRES ARE BLUE — AMETHYSTS ARE PURPLE — GOLD IS YELLOW

HINTS FOR COLORING

BRACELETS

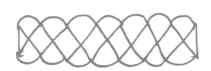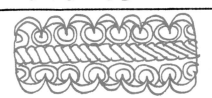

55

ETC...

ETC.

ETC.

ETC.

ALSO......

HARRY

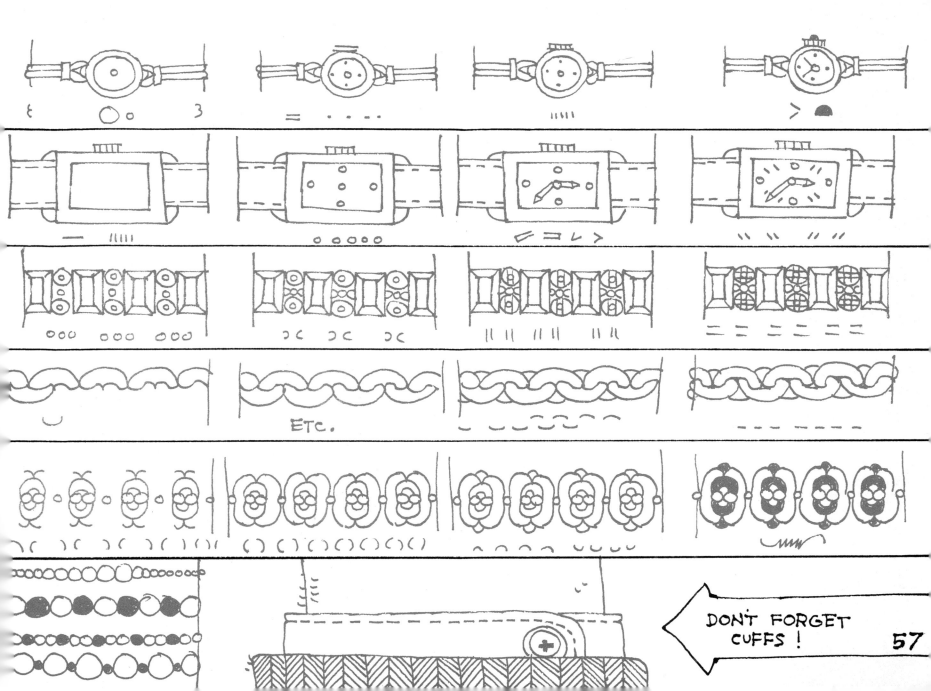

ETC.

DON'T FORGET CUFFS!

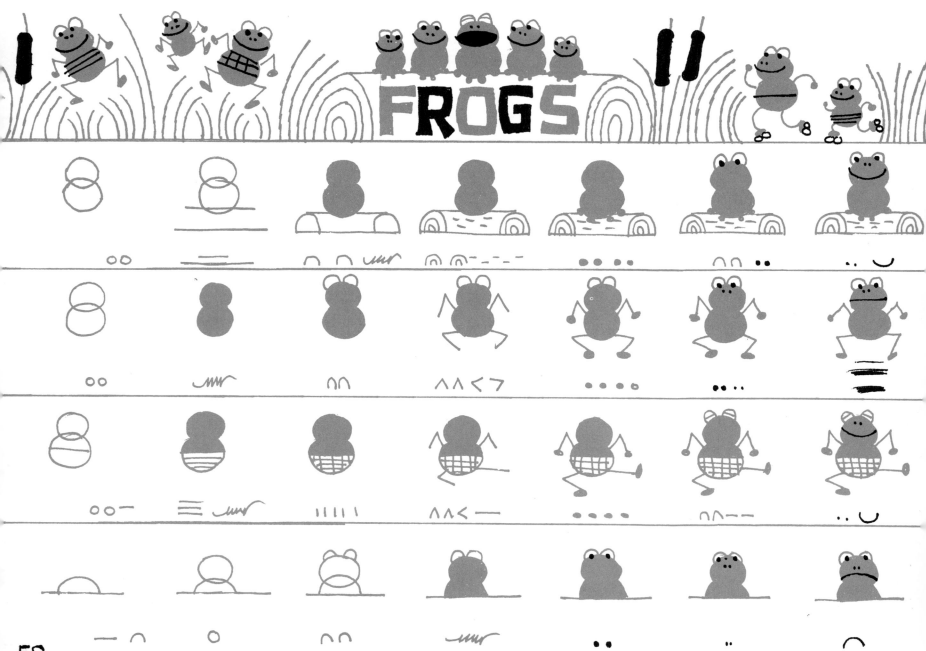

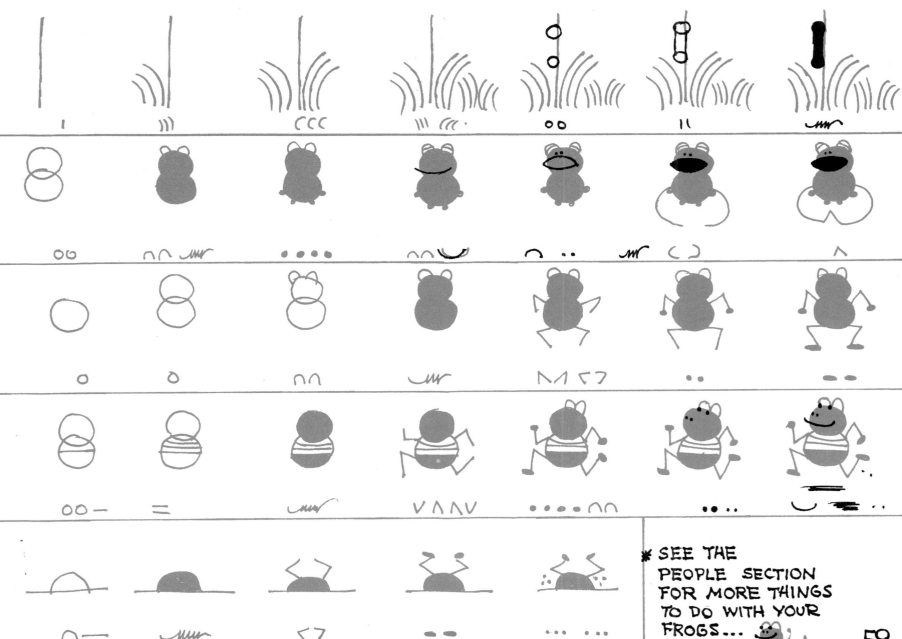

* SEE THE PEOPLE SECTION FOR MORE THINGS TO DO WITH YOUR FROGS...

59

4¢ KOALA

I USED A
PENNY TO
MAKE THE
CIRCLES FOR
THIS PICTURE

 o 1¢

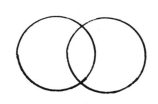 o 2¢

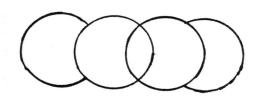

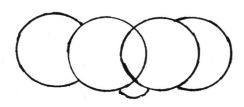

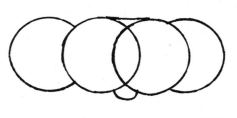

o 3¢ o 4¢

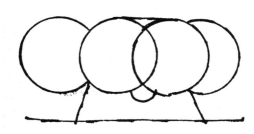

60

GREENGRIN

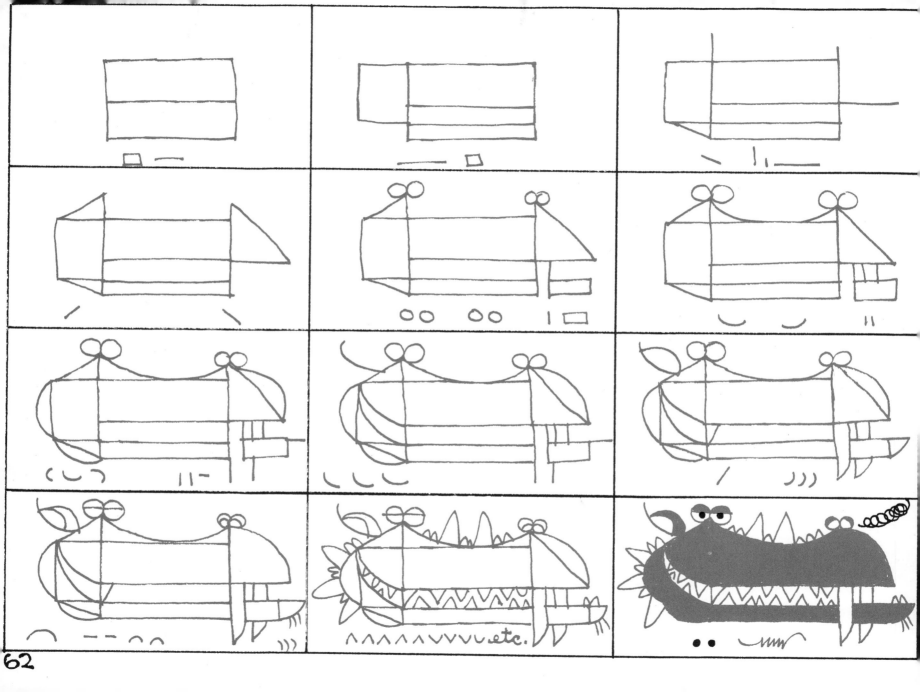

63

64

DR. JEKYLL

AND THEN...

FIRST THE POTION...

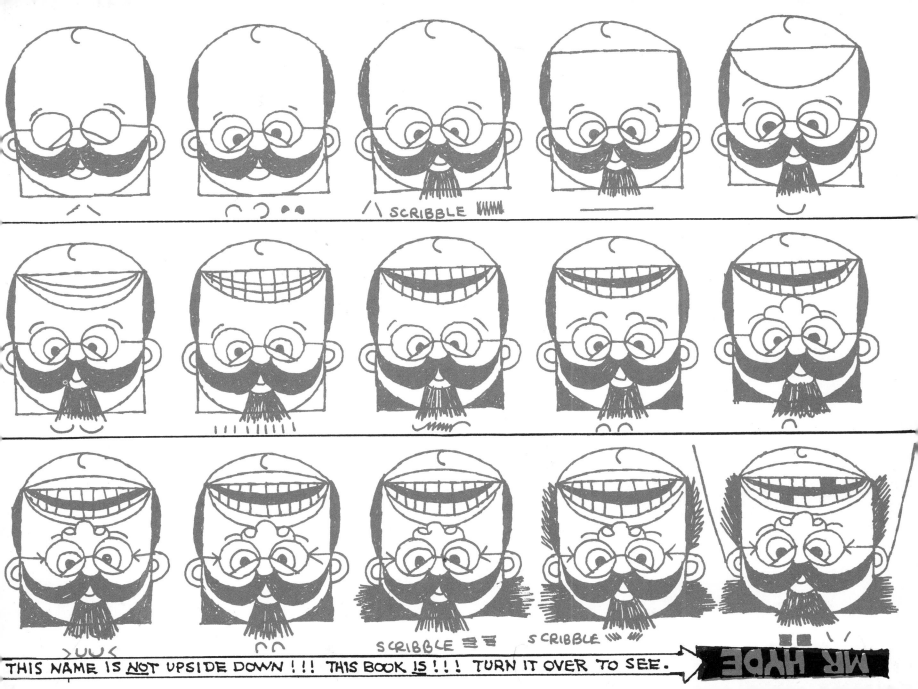

SCRIBBLE

SCRIBBLE

SCRIBBLE

THIS NAME IS <u>NOT</u> UPSIDE DOWN !!! THIS BOOK <u>IS</u> !!! TURN IT OVER TO SEE.

MR HYDE

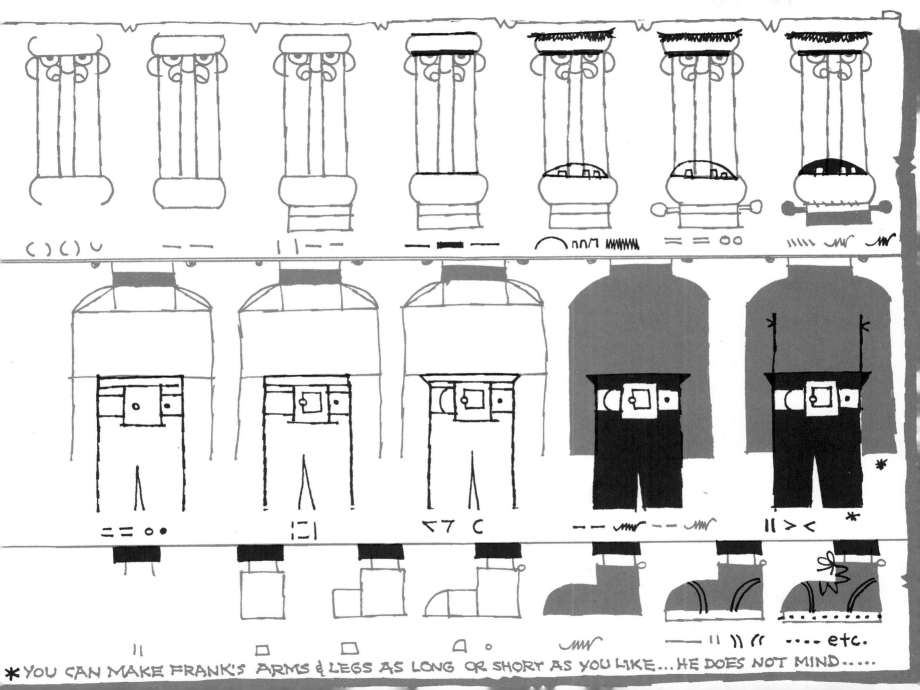

* YOU CAN MAKE FRANK'S ARMS & LEGS AS LONG OR SHORT AS YOU LIKE... HE DOES NOT MIND.....

DRACULA

68

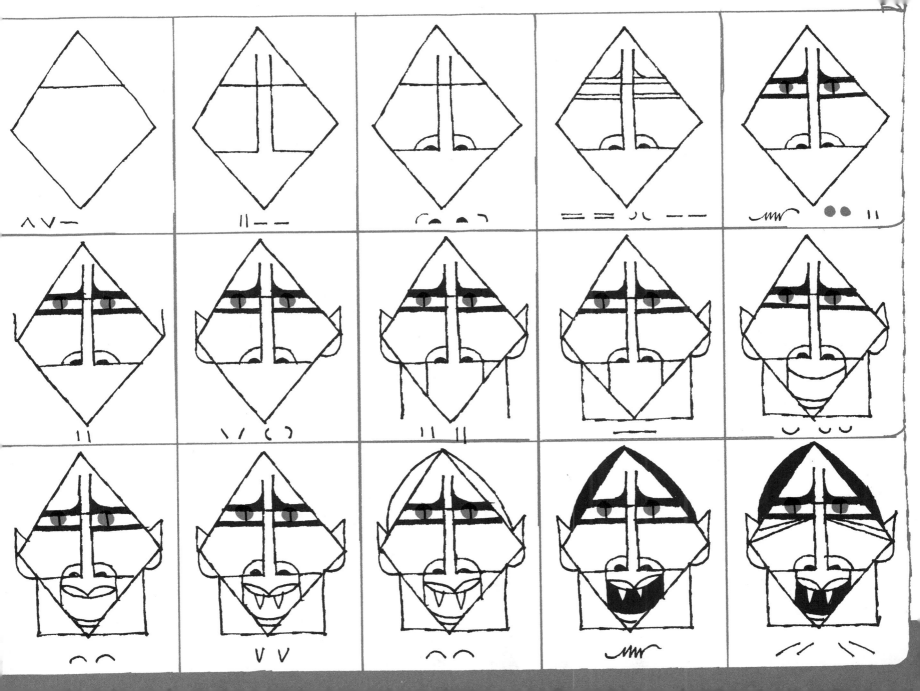

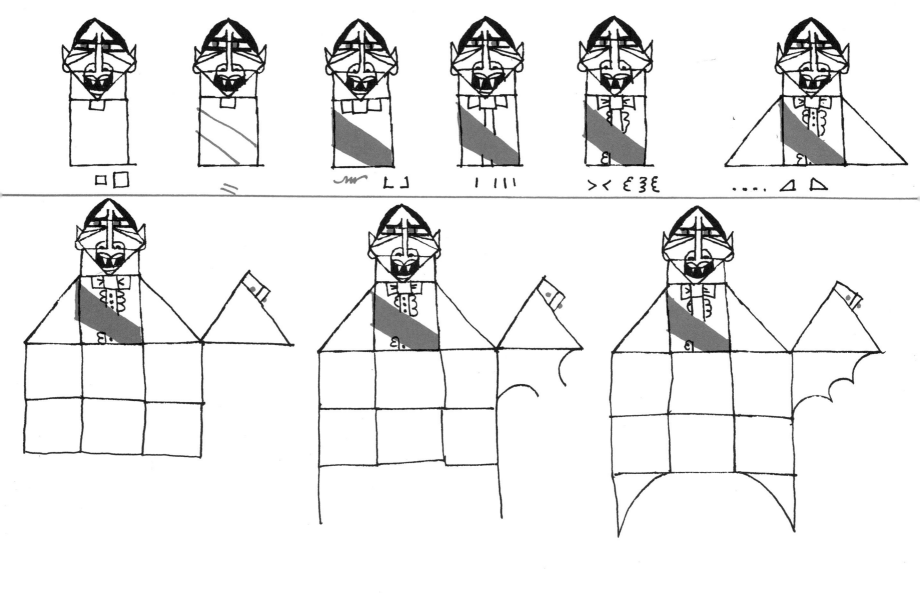

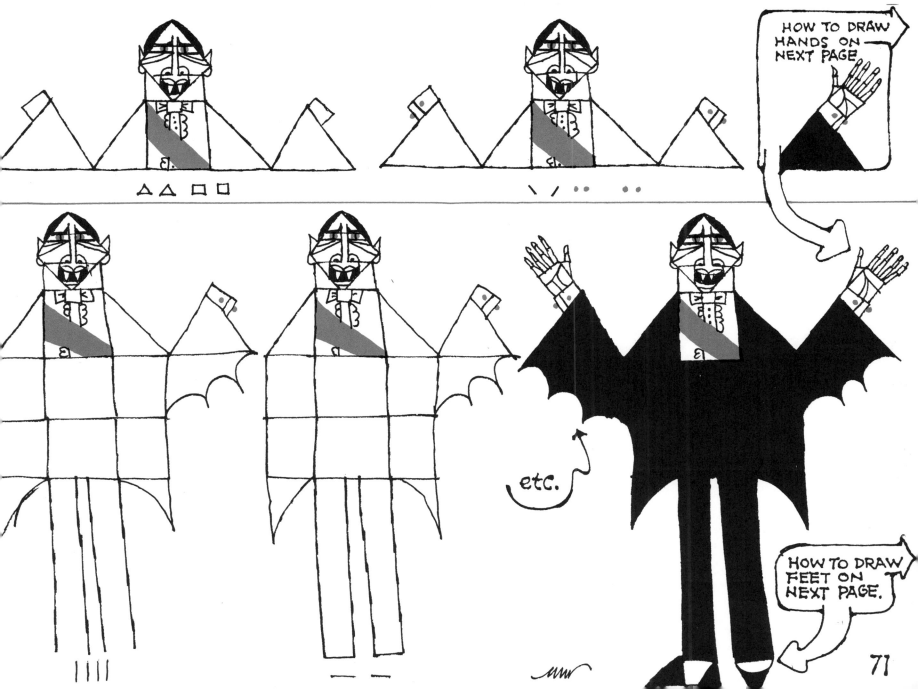

HOW TO DRAW HANDS ON NEXT PAGE

△ △ □ □

\ / •• ••

etc.

HOW TO DRAW FEET ON NEXT PAGE.

71

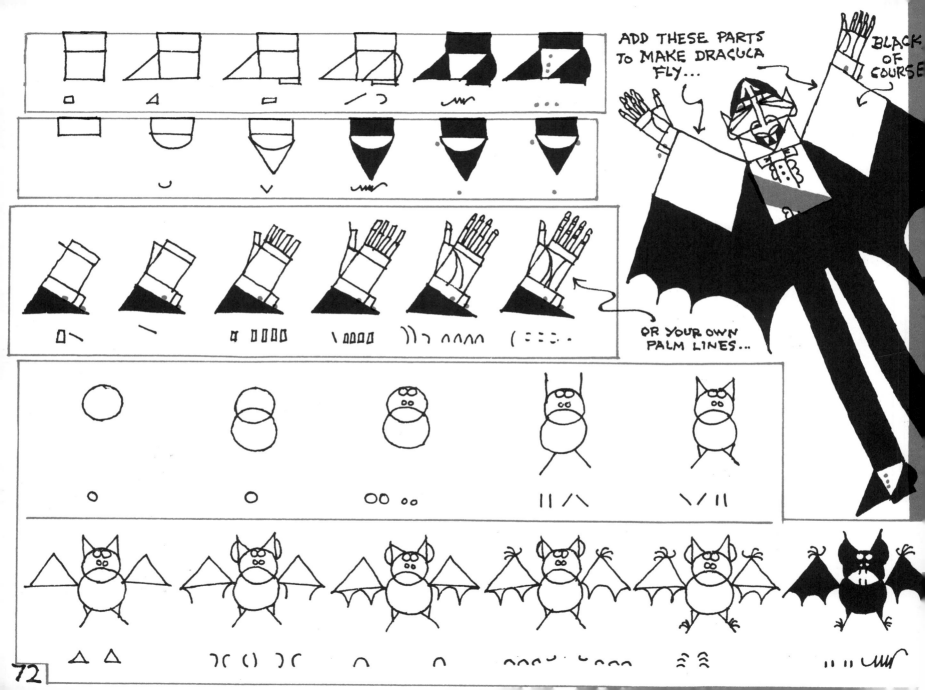

ADD THESE PARTS TO MAKE DRACULA FLY...

BLACK OF COURSE

OR YOUR OWN PALM LINES...

DRACULA'S CAR

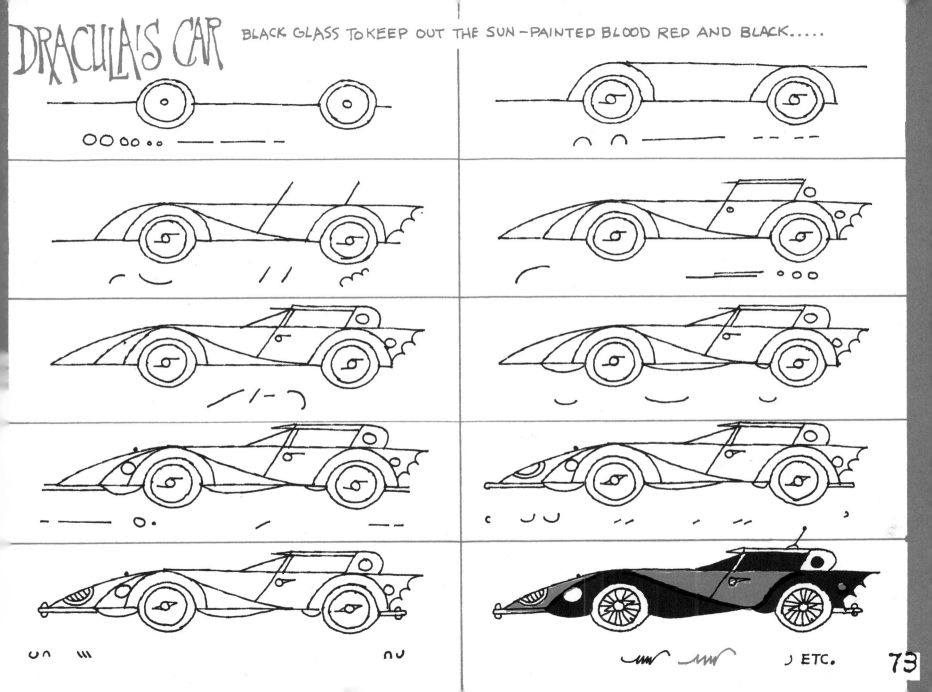

ETC.

73

HERE ARE SOME WAYS YOU CAN USE SCRIBBLES TO MAKE TREES, BUSHES, FORESTS, JUNGLES, GARDENS, PARKS, ETC.

74

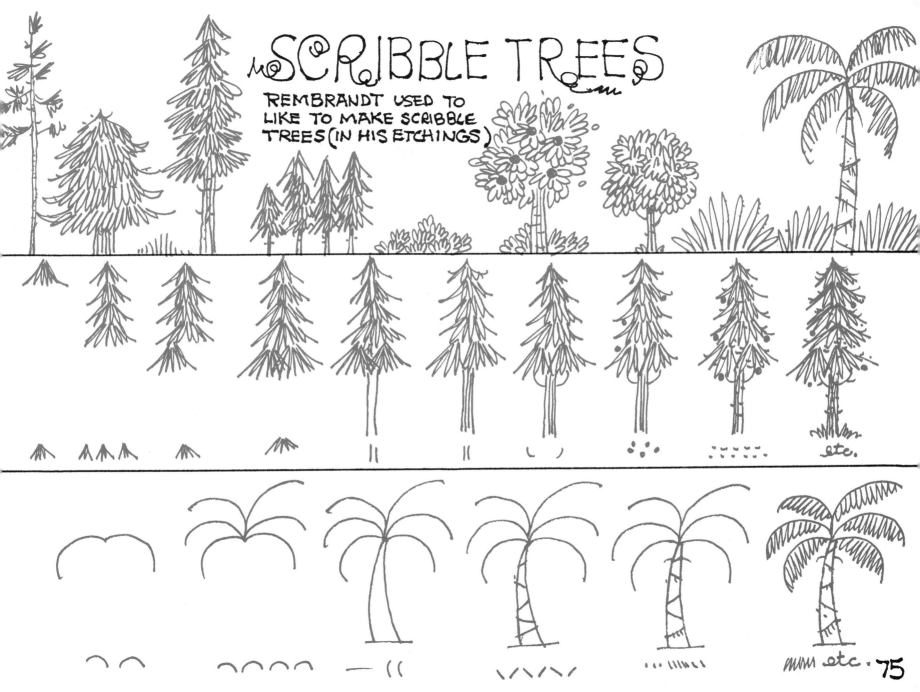

SCRIBBLE TREES

REMBRANDT USED TO
LIKE TO MAKE SCRIBBLE
TREES (IN HIS ETCHINGS)

etc.

etc.

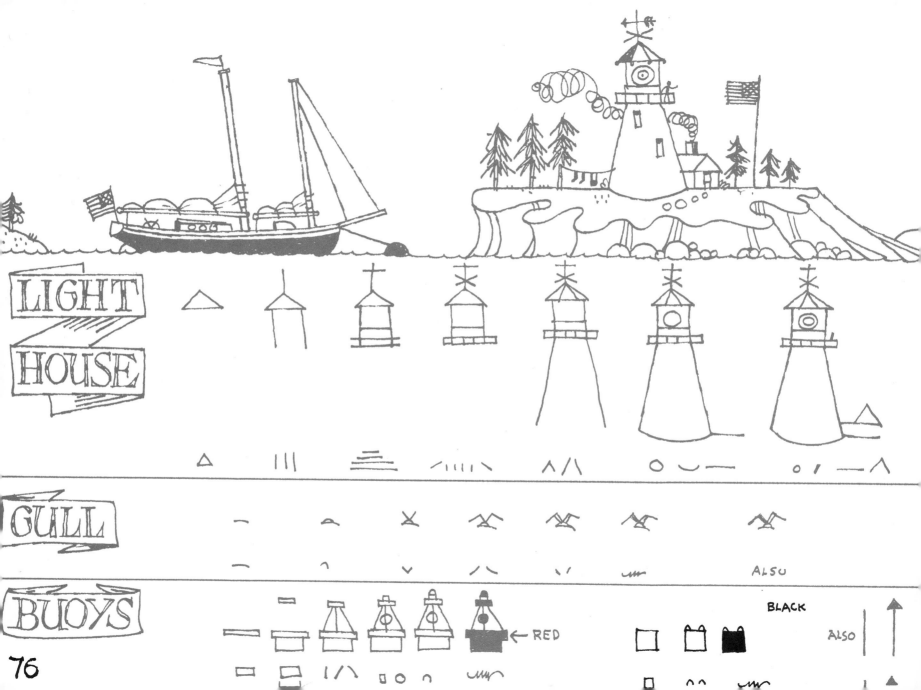

LIGHT HOUSE

GULL

ALSO

BUOYS

← RED

BLACK

ALSO

76

PINE ISLAND

YAWL BOAT
Nellie

ISLAND

CLIFFS

78

ALSO

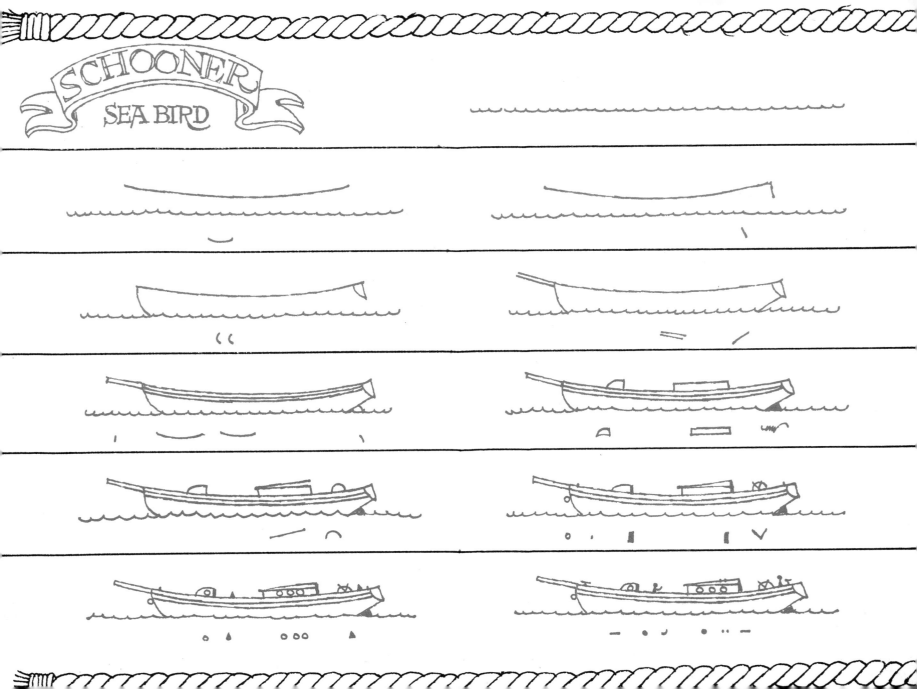

SCHOONER
SEA BIRD

AT ANCHOR

FILL IN

CLIPPER BOW SCHOONER — MATTIE II.

3 MASTED SCHOONER — EAGLE

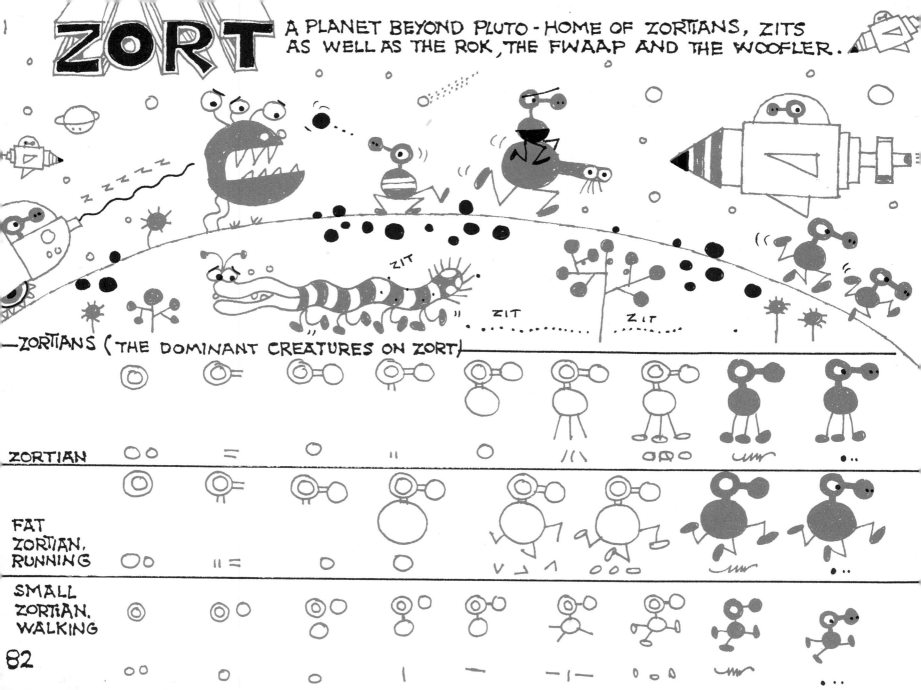

ZORT

A PLANET BEYOND PLUTO - HOME OF ZORTIANS, ZITS AS WELL AS THE ROK, THE FWAAP AND THE WOOFLER...

ZIT

ZIT   ZIT

ZORTIANS (THE DOMINANT CREATURES ON ZORT)

ZORTIAN

FAT ZORTIAN. RUNNING

SMALL ZORTIAN. WALKING

82

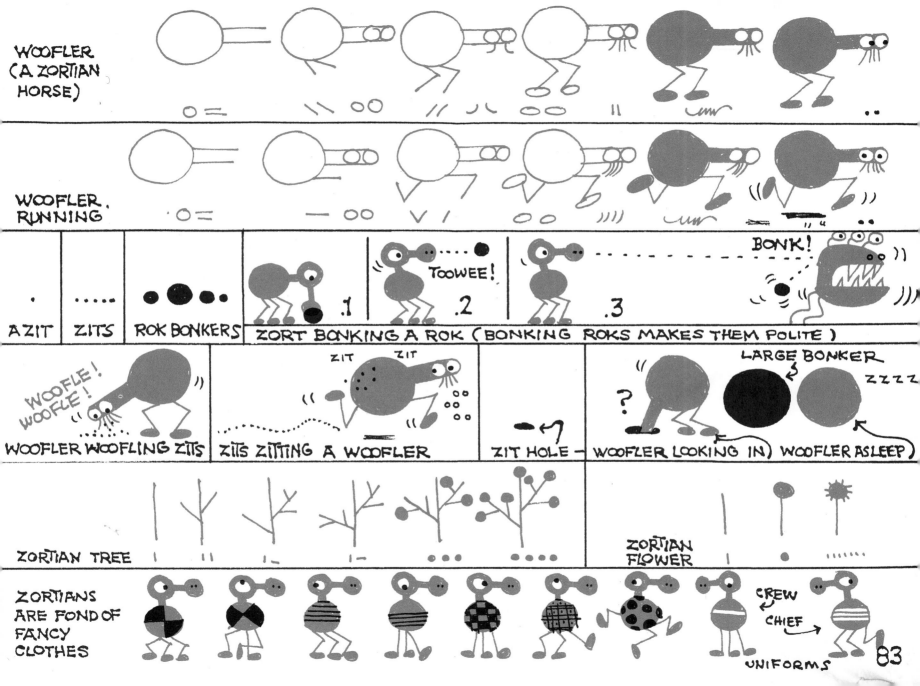

WOOFLER
(A ZORTIAN
HORSE)

WOOFLER,
RUNNING

A ZIT | ZITS | ROK BONKERS | ZORT BONKING A ROK (BONKING ROKS MAKES THEM POLITE)

.1 TOOWEE! .2 .3 BONK!

WOOFLE!
WOOFLE!

WOOFLER WOOFLING ZITS | ZIT ZIT ZITS ZITTING A WOOFLER | ZIT HOLE — | WOOFLER LOOKING IN) LARGE BONKER ZZZZ WOOFLER ASLEEP)

ZORTIAN TREE

ZORTIAN
FLOWER

ZORTIANS
ARE FOND OF
FANCY
CLOTHES

CREW
CHIEF

UNIFORMS

83

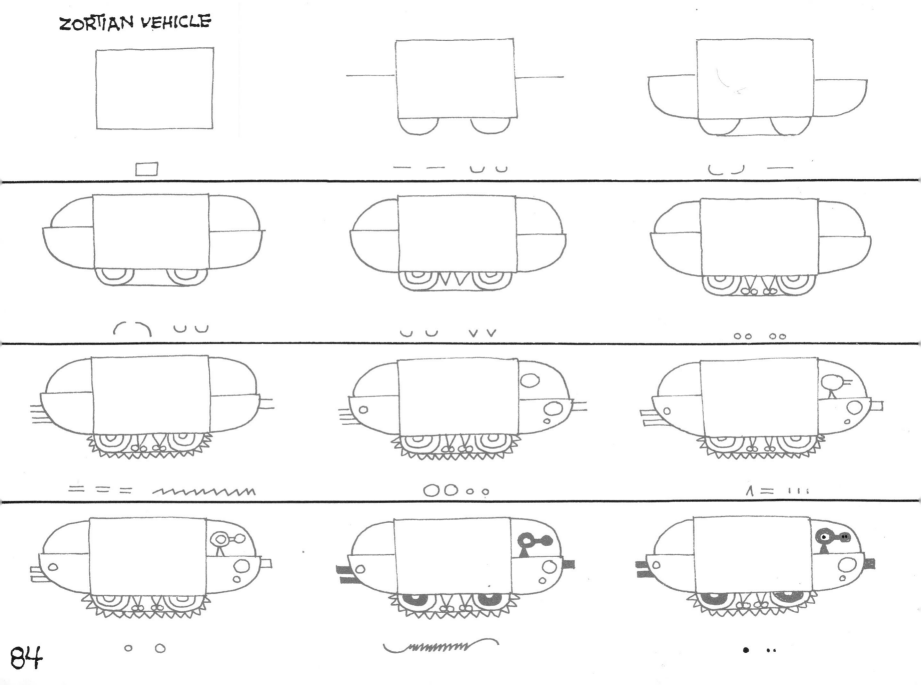

ZORTIAN VEHICLE

84

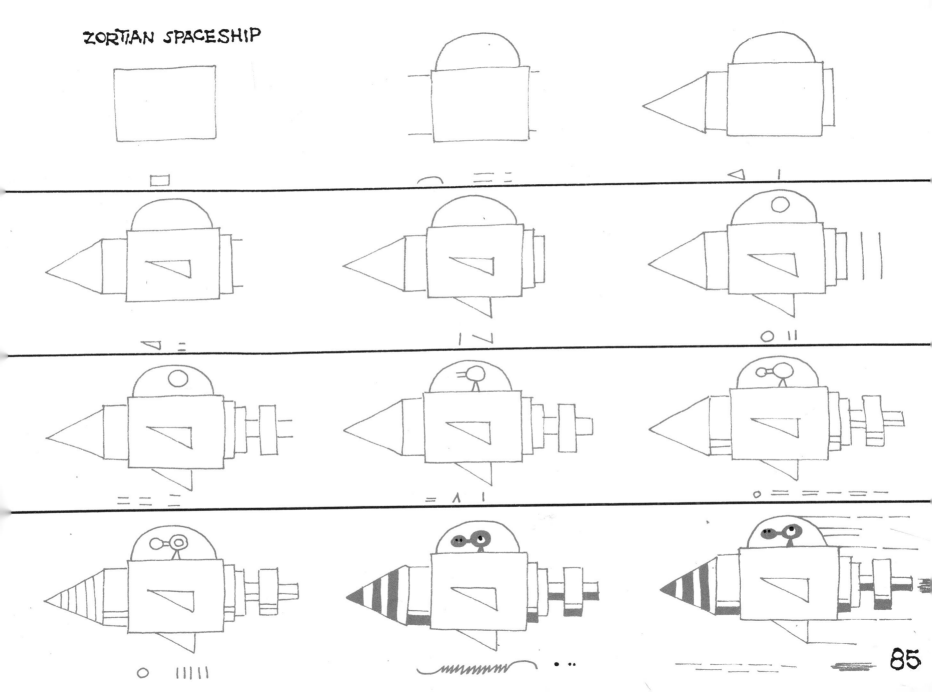

ZORTIAN SPACESHIP

85

ZORTIAN COMMAND SHIP

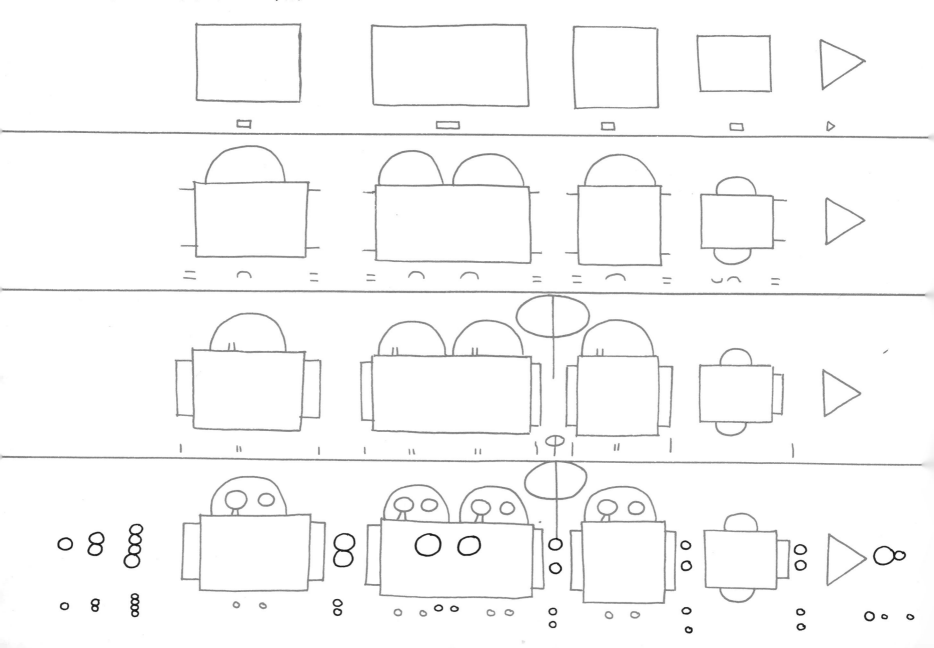

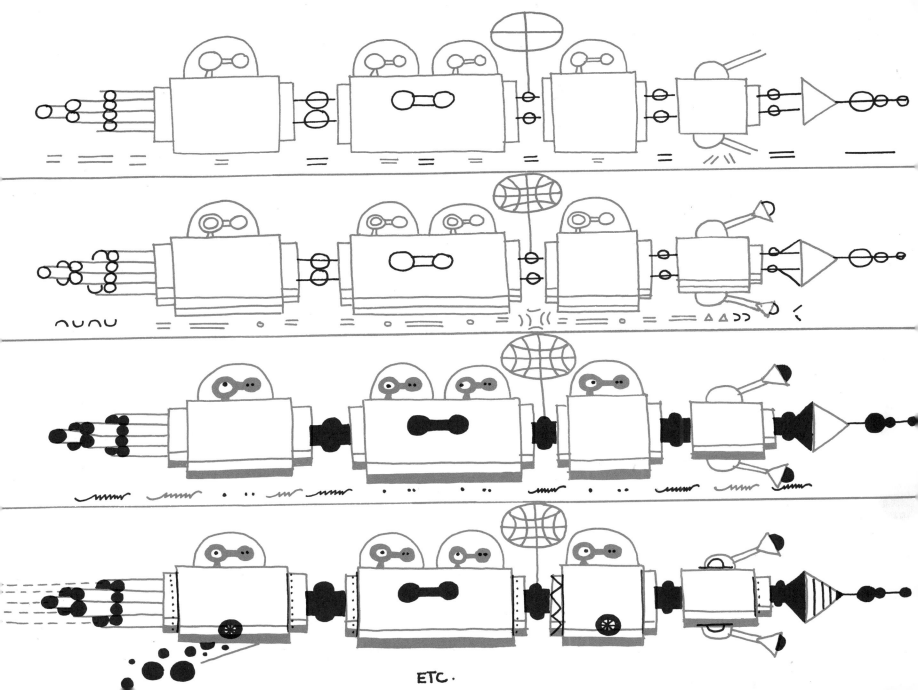

ETC.

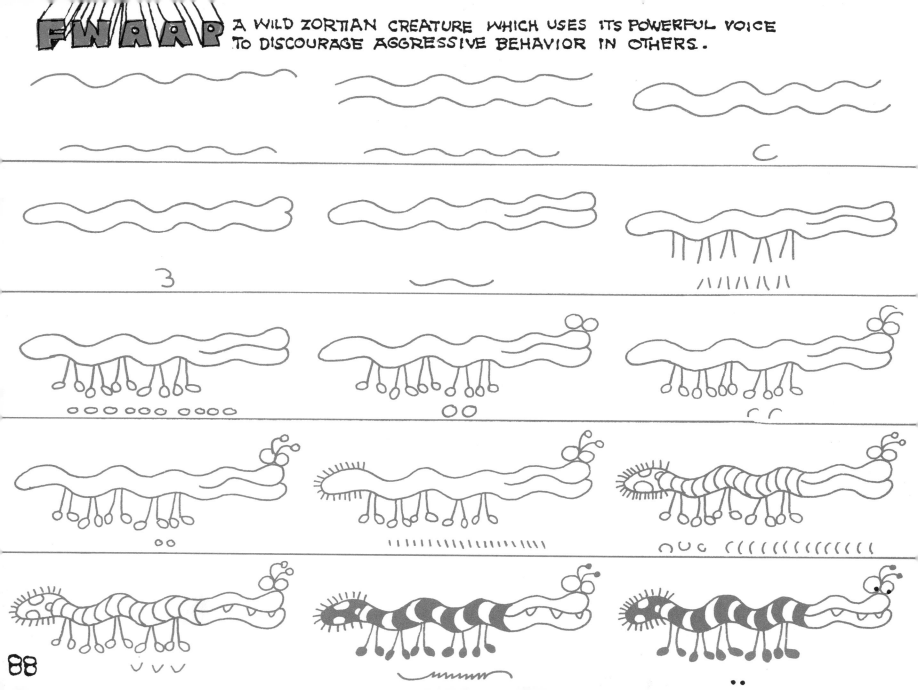

FWAAP A WILD ZORTIAN CREATURE WHICH USES ITS POWERFUL VOICE TO DISCOURAGE AGGRESSIVE BEHAVIOR IN OTHERS.

A FWAAP SAYING "FWAAP"! A STRONG "FWAAP" CAN DISCOURAGE EVEN THE UNPLEASANT ROK.

ROK

THE ROK IS ZORT'S MOST UNFRIENDLY CREATURE.

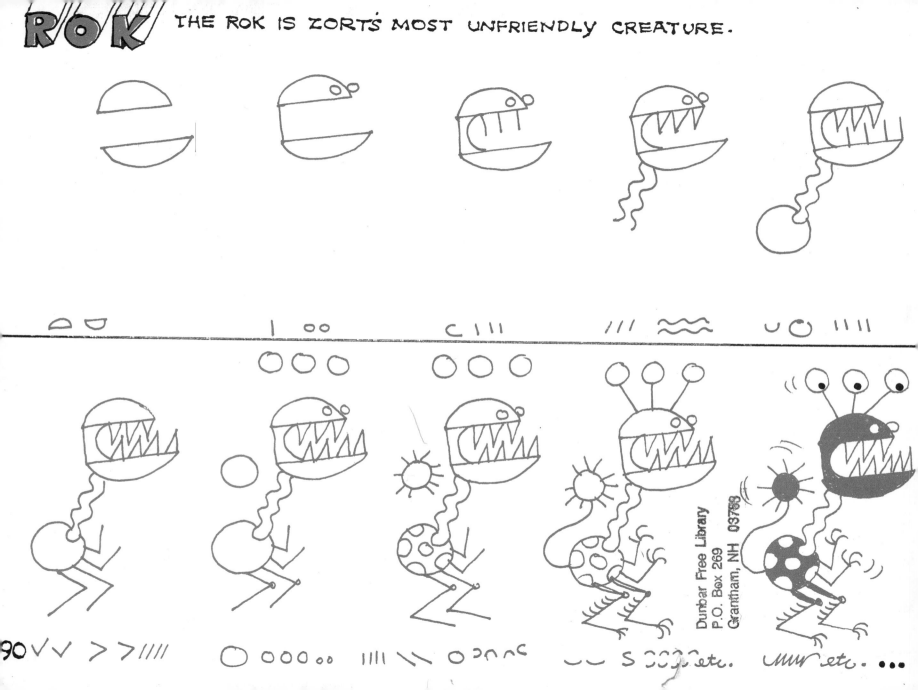

90